Human Rights Watch

Human Rights Watch is composed of Africa Watch, Americas Watch, Asia Watch, Helsinki Watch, Middle East Watch and the Fund for Free Expression.

The executive committee comprises Robert L. Bernstein, chair; Adrian DeWind, vice chair; Roland Algrant, Lisa Anderson, Peter Bell, Alice Brown, William Carmichael, Dorothy Cullman, Irene Diamond, Jonathan Fanton, Jack Greenberg, Alice H. Henkin, Stephen Kass, Marina Kaufman, Jeri Laber, Aryeh Neier, Bruce Rabb, Harriet Rabb, Kenneth Roth, Orville Schell, Gary Sick, and Robert Wedgeworth.

The staff includes Aryeh Neier, executive director; Kenneth Roth, deputy director; Holly J. Burkhalter, Washington director; Ellen Lutz, California director; Susan Osnos, press director; Jemera Rone, counsel; Joanna Weschler, Prison Project director; Kenneth Anderson, Arms Project director; and Dorothy Q. Thomas, Women's Rights Project director.

Executive Directors

Africa Watch	Americas Watch Juan E. Méndez	Asia Watch Sidney Jones
Helsinki Watch Jeri Laber	Middle East Watch Andrew Whitley	Fund for Free Expression Gara LaMarche

Adresses for Human Rights Watch and its Divisions

485 Fifth Avenue
New York, NY 10017
Tel: (212) 972-8400
Fax: (212) 972-0905

1522 K Street, NW, #910
Washington, DC 20005
Tel: (202) 371-6592
Fax: (202) 371-0124

10951 West Pico Blvd., #203
Los Angeles, CA 90064
Tel: (213) 475-3070
Fax: (213) 475-5613

90 Borough High Street
London, UK SE1 1LL
Tel: (071) 378-8008
Fax: (071) 378-8029

TABLE OF CONTENTS

ACKNOWLEDGMENTS

This report is based primarily on information gathered during the inspection of six Egyptian prisons in February 1992 by Virginia N. Sherry, associate director of Middle East Watch, and John Valery White, an attorney and Orville Schell Fellow with Human Rights Watch.

The report was written by Ms. Sherry, with parts contributed by Mr. White. Joanna Weschler, the director of the Prison Project of Human Rights Watch, and Aryeh Neier, the executive director of Human Rights Watch, edited the report.

Suzanne Howard skillfully prepared this manuscript for publication.

*   *   *

We extend our appreciation to the prison commanders and their staffs who accompanied us during the inspections and who were consistently cordial and responsive to our numerous queries and requests.

We wish to thank the prisoners and detainees—Egyptian, Palestinian, Lebanese, Sudanese, Nigerian, Pakistani, and American—who chose to speak with us, often in the presence or view of officials. Without the cooperation of these men and women, this report would not have been possible.

We also express our thanks to the Egyptian and foreign prisoners who wrote letters to Middle East Watch in 1992 about their conditions of confinement. We have included relevant information from some of these letters; unfortunately, their complaints about the administration of justice in Egyptian courts are beyond the scope of this report.

ACRONYMS AND ARABIC TERMS

Central Security Forces:
> The Egyptian paramilitary force of some 300,000 troops used for internal-security functions; the force was formed in 1977.

EOHR: Egyptian Organization for Human Rights, the independent, Cairo-based human rights monitoring organization.

foul: Fava beans, a staple of the Egyptian diet.

istikbal: "reception" in Arabic. Tora Istikbal, one of the six prisons at the complex at Tora, was designed as a reception prison. It functions today as a major holding center for suspected Islamist security detainees, held short term (several months) and long term (several years).

liman: The Arabic term used to describe Egypt's three maximum-security prisons: Abu Za'bal Liman, Tora Liman, and Wadi Natroun Liman.

niyaba: The term widely used by Egyptians to describe the niyaba al-'amma, part of the Ministry of Justice. The niyaba is "an institution taken directly from the French legal system....There is no counterpart in the common law systems of England and the United States, although parallels are often noted. These officials of the magistery not only prepare and present the charges against an accused to the full session of the criminal court, but they have various functions in line with their prescribed duty to 'protect the public interest' which, especially in Egypt, amounts to an almost unfettered authority to conduct investigations....

"The personnel of the niyaba are often translated as 'attorney general,' 'district attorney,' or 'prosecuting attorney,' but these are misappellations. The niyaba neither represents the government as a party litigant nor is its function, strictly speaking, to 'prosecute' cases in the sense that prosecution is conceived of in America or England.

"The niyaba is the place where incidents are investigated, proving the background of evidence, and serving as a supporting organ which seeks to learn the 'truth' and not to incriminate for the sake of having a case. They search for all evidence—of innocence as well as guilt. They have the authority to suspend investigations and 'file' cases, as well as to recommend that a case be brought to trial. The individual who is given the task of preparing the charges for presentation to the criminal court may well be another individual than the one who was in charge of the investigation, indeed, he likely is, as all reports of investigations must be submitted to the superior officers of the niyaba, and then redistributed for preparation for trial....Any of the personnel are interchangeable in the performance of the responsibilities which devolve upon the niyaba."[1]

State Security Investigation, or SSI:

One of Egypt's three intelligence organizations. SSI is part of the Ministry of Interior and is said to be under the direct control of the Minister of Interior.

---

[1]Enid Hill, *Mahkama! Studies in the Egyptian Legal System/Courts & Crimes, Law & Society* (Ithaca Press, London: 1979), pp. 26-28.

PREFACE

This is the first report by a human-rights organization about Egyptian prisons based on on-site inspections. Beginning on February 12, 1992, Middle East Watch inspected six prisons in an eight-day period. These facilities housed approximately 9,800 inmates, over twenty-seven percent of Egypt's prison population. Five of the prisons are located just outside the Cairo metropolitan area: the maximum-security prison at Abu Za'bal, northeast of the city; the women's prison in Qanater, northwest of Cairo; and three prisons in the Tora complex southeast of Cairo—Tora Istikbal, Tora Mazraa and the maximum-security Tora Liman. The sixth facility inspected was the general prison and women's jail in Tanta, a city fifty-five miles northwest of the capital.

The Egyptian government must be credited for making this independent investigation possible. The authorities granted Middle East Watch permission to visit prisons of our choice and—equally important—provided unimpeded access at five of the six institutions that we selected for inspection. As discussed below, access was significantly curbed only at Tora Istikbal, the prison where some 400 Islamist security detainees[2] were being held without charge, some of them for several years.

This report is one of a series in which Human Rights Watch, through its Prison Project, has investigated conditions in prisons worldwide. To date, reports have been published on Brazil, Czechoslovakia, India, Indonesia, Israel and the Israeli-occupied territories, Jamaica, Mexico, Poland, Romania, Spain, Turkey, the former Soviet Union, the United Kingdom and the United States. A report on prison conditions in South Africa will be published later this year.

Since 1990, Middle East Watch had sought permission from the Egyptian authorities to inspect prisons, but these efforts were

---

[2]Throughout this report, we use the terms "security detainees" or "security prisoners" to refer to those individuals incarcerated in reprisal for peaceful political expression and association as well as those who may have been incarcerated for politically motivated crimes. These terms and definitions are those that have been long used by the International Committee of the Red Cross.

unsuccessful. In May 1990, a team representing Middle East Watch, the Prison Project of Human Rights Watch and the Boston-based Physicians for Human Rights organization, spent ten days in Egypt, interviewing released prisoners and defense lawyers, but was denied access to prisons. Prior to the mission, numerous letters had been sent to government ministers, including Interior Minister General Abdel Halim Moussa, accepting an open invitation to foreign observers from the then newly appointed official to inspect Egyptian prisons. Efforts to persuade the authorities in Cairo to fulfill their own offer included a personal letter from former U.S. President Jimmy Carter to President Hosni Mubarak.

On December 23, 1991, Middle East Watch informed the government of plans to conduct a mission to investigate torture and detention. Among other requests, we asked again for access to the prisons. By the time the delegation arrived in Egypt in late January 1992, meetings with government officials had been approved but there was no word about the request to visit prisons.

On February 5, 1992, the tenth day of the mission, we were informed during a meeting with Egypt's Prosecutor General, Chancellor Raga el-Araby, that permission to inspect prisons had been granted and that we could visit any of the country's thirty prisons. Because the governmental response came late during our stay in Egypt, constraints of our schedule limited the inspections to six prisons; the authorities, however, had made it clear that we could visit as many prisons as we wished.

At each of the prisons inspected, we interviewed prison officials, sentenced criminal and security prisoners, administrative detainees, and prisoners awaiting trial or in trial proceedings. We met several times with Gen. Mahmoud Fakarani, the director of the Prisons Administration, and members of his staff. In January and February 1992, we also interviewed former prisoners, lawyers, human rights monitors and others in Alexandria, Assyut, Aswan, Cairo, Mansoura and Minya.

THE NATURE OF THE ACCESS

In five of the six facilities visited, access was excellent. We were allowed to enter and inspect any section of any prison, including living quarters, punishment wings, and hospitals. The authorities complied with requests to open locked doors in randomly selected areas. Even though Chancellor el-Araby had warned us that prisons closed at dark, and individual prison commanders emphasized that their prisons closed at 2:00 p.m., we were allowed to remain at several prisons after 4:00 p.m., and remained at one prison until 7:00 p.m., well after dark.

RESTRICTED ACCESS AT TORA ISTIKBAL PRISON

Our access was significantly limited by the authorities at Tora Istikbal prison, where most of Egypt's unsentenced security prisoners were being held. Unlike the experience at other prisons, we encountered delays and obstacles in gaining admission to this prison. Once inside the facility, we were allowed to inspect only one of the prison's two main buildings, and permitted less than one hour in the cell area. (In fact, the prison commander actively discouraged us from even entering the cell area. Explaining that the detainees were "dangerous," he said that he could not guarantee our safety and that we would have to proceed at our own risk.) The prison commander also denied our repeated requests to visit an area of the prison nicknamed "The Hospital," an improvised punishment wing where alleged leaders of radical Islamic groups have been held continuously, one of them for over three years (see Chapter Four).

We had initially asked to inspect Tora Istikbal on February 12, 1992, but the director of the Prisons Administration, Gen. Mahmoud Fakarani, said that it was preferable to visit the maximum-security prison at Abu Za'bal first, which we did. When we arrived at the Tora prison complex the next day, we were strongly encouraged to visit Tora Liman, the maximum-security prison there, before visiting nearby Tora Istikbal. The inspection of Tora Liman took all day, and officials said that a visit to Tora Istikbal could be scheduled for later the next week.

We were scheduled to meet a senior officer from the Prisons Administration at Qanater women's prison on February 15; it had been agreed that at this time a date would be arranged for the inspection of Tora Istikbal. When the officer did not meet us at Qanater, we decided to forego a scheduled visit to another prison on February 16 and visit Tora Istikbal unannounced. We had reason to believe that officials were trying to keep us out of Tora Istikbal because we had heard rumors that a hunger strike by security detainees was in progress.

When we arrived at Tora Istikbal at 9:00 a.m. on February 16, we were taken to nearby Tora Liman prison, where officials had us wait for over four hours. They eventually confirmed that indeed a hunger strike was in progress at Tora Istikbal, but provided varying accounts about the strike's scope and duration.[3] When we finally entered the prison, the authorities permitted only forty-five minutes to inspect Building A (a four-story dormitory) and interview prisoners. The building was ringing with the chants and rhythmic banging on metal cell doors which the striking prisoners began as soon as they were aware that we were inside. Prison officers repeatedly said that the protest was being staged for our benefit.

We were allowed to enter locked cells, talk privately with detainees, and keep handwritten petitions that the prisoners gave us (see Appendix). Officials insisted, however, that we leave the building at 2:00 p.m. After leaving, we met with the commander of Tora Istikbal, Gen. Muhammad Awad, and other officials. During this one-hour meeting, banging and chanting by the striking prisoners started and ended, in

---

[3] One senior security officer told us that the strike began the day before our visit, on February 15. Minutes later, he said that the strike was in its fifth day and had started on February 12. "They knew you were at Abu Za'bal Liman on [February 12] and they started the strike on [February 12]." This officer also said that there were slightly over 200 prisoners on strike, although a higher-ranking officer and the director of the Prisons Administration later told us that virtually all of the 400 security detainees at Tora Istikbal were striking.

The commander of the Tora prisons complex gave still other reasons for the strike and a different starting date: "There is a strike going on only because the inmates knew you were coming. When you left Tora Liman [on February 13], they [the other prisoners] told them you were coming back." When challenged on whether the strike grew out of our visit to Abu Za'bal two days earlier, the commander conceded that the strike started before that. He told us that it had originated when the detainees read Egyptian newspaper accounts about our prison visits. (*See* Middle East Watch, "Arrest and Detention Practices and Prison Conditions," March 1992, for information about Egyptian pro-government daily newspapers' coverage of our prison inspections.)

concert, several times. Gen. Awad denied our request to visit "The Hospital," saying that "the chanting and noise will not end until you are gone." He promised that we could inspect "The Hospital" on a return visit two days later. However, when we did return, we were denied access to Tora Istikbal. When asked the reasons for the denial, prison officials were initially evasive, offering varying and contradictory security justifications. Ultimately, the commander of the Tora prisons complex flatly denied us access.

INTERVIEWS WITH PRISONERS

During the inspections, the authorities permitted us to speak with prisoners and spend extended periods of time with groups of security prisoners. In addition, when we supplied the names of individual prisoners with whom we wished to speak, officials either had the prisoners brought to us or told us where they were being held. We were allowed us to talk with them inside their cells, with the door closed and the guards out of earshot.

Many inmates, especially sentenced criminal prisoners, were not eager to speak to us. The large entourage of prison officials and guards that typically accompanied us during inspections clearly raised suspicions for some prisoners and frightened others, thereby limiting their candor. Until we could speak privately with prisoners about the purpose of the visit, it was not at all clear to them, from first appearances, why foreign visitors were inside the prison and the nature of their relationship to the authorities. In fact, everywhere we went, inmates appeared surprised—or shocked—by the presence of outsiders. Criminal prisoners often stood at attention and saluted when we entered their cells, even if we were unaccompanied by prison officials or guards. Some inmates expressed fear that they might be subjected to reprisals for talking to us.

INTIMIDATION OF WOMEN PRISONERS

At Qanater women's prison, officers and guards entered a crowded dormitory cell immediately after one member of the delegation had conducted an interview with a sentenced prisoner. The officers were heard shouting at the women. After learning of this incident, the second delegation member returned to the cell later, and sought out the woman who had spoken freely. Angered by what had happened, and shielded from the view of guards and prison officials by other inmates, she said: "The guards came in and took and tore up [the first MEW representative's] business cards. They asked me what I said and didn't say. I told them that I didn't say anything."

OTHER FORMS OF INTERFERENCE

Some prison officials and guards, who did not interrupt our work but appeared visibly disturbed by our presence, attempted to look in on interviews or, if they could hear some of the questions, coach answers or offer responses. Furthermore, interviews with prisoners in large, crowded cells made open conversation difficult. Prisoners were understandably apprehensive, and we could not be sure that there were no informants monitoring those who spoke freely.

At Tanta general prison, for example, we feared that conversations with prisoners were being monitored by either "trustees" (collaborators or informants) or guards dressed as inmates. When we entered one small cell where six men were being held, a seventh man stepped into the previously locked cell after we had entered. This man, whom we had seen earlier in the building's atrium courtyard, was dressed, untypically, in a new-looking, clean and pressed dark blue prisoner's uniform. When asked, he indicated that he did not live in the cell, and left when requested.

In a transfer cell on the first floor of the same building, two men, also clad in clean new prison uniforms, repeatedly offered answers to questions that we asked of some of their twenty-two cellmates. These two men, who wore sneakers rather than the typical sandals, continued to answer questions directed at others, even after we repeatedly requested that they stop interrupting the interviews. The other prisoners in the cell were visibly frightened. On occasions such as this, we limited interviews so as not to place prisoners at risk.

THE HUMAN RIGHTS STANDARDS APPLIED IN THE REPORT

As in the other reports on prison conditions issued by the Prison Project and other regional divisions of Human Rights Watch, in this report Middle East Watch assesses the Egyptian government's practices in accordance with the guidelines set forth in the United Nations Standard Minimum Rules for the Treatment of Prisoners, as well as those in international human-rights treaties to which Egypt is a state party. We also hold the authorities to the standards enshrined in the Egyptian Constitution and to the guarantees set down in Egyptian laws and administrative regulations.

A Note About Measurements

Throughout this report, the dimensions noted for cells, windows and courtyards are approximate, based on visual observation and not precise measurement.

INTRODUCTION

Some conditions in Egypt's prisons have changed little over the past half-century. In January 1946, future president Anwar Sadat was arrested at his home in the middle of the night, brought to the Aliens' Jail in Cairo, and placed in solitary confinement for a week before being interrogated. After complaining to the public prosecutor about intimidation and torture, Sadat was transferred to Cairo central prison, where he was held for eighteen months. His description of the conditions in Cell Fifty-Four could have been written today:

> [T]here was no bed, no small table, no chair, and no lamp. It was completely bare—apart from a palm-fiber mat on the macadamized floor, hardly big enough for a man to sleep on, and an unbelievably dirty blanket. You simply can't imagine how filthy that thing was. In the winter water oozed from the cell walls day and night, and in the summer huge armies of bugs marched up and down.

Sadat in 1946 endured the same appalling sanitary conditions, and limited time outside his cell, that prisoners continue to experience:

> We were initially allowed a daily break of a mere fifteen minutes, for a "solitary" walk. After the referring magistrate had examined our case, we were given two breaks a day, of forty-five minutes each—one in the morning, the other in the afternoon—during which we were allowed to see one another and talk. Our conversations dealt mostly with our ordeal in that terrible jail, particularly the incredibly dirty toilets. Apart from their unhygienic condition (which made them unfit for human use), we had to use them "collectively"...you had toilets designed for, say, a thousand but always crammed with three thousand.[1]

---

[1] Anwar el-Sadat, *In Search of Identity: An Autobiography* (Harper & Row, New York: 1977), pp. 68-69.

Despite the overthrow of the monarchy in 1952, the various commitments to reform proclaimed by the successive regimes of Nasser, Sadat himself and Mubarak, and Egypt's ratification of international human-rights accords, prison conditions remain abysmal in significant respects.

One underlying problem is that Egyptian prisons are controlled by the Ministry of Interior, which has long been implicated in human-rights abuses, including torture and prolonged detention without trial.[2] Under Egypt's long-standing emergency law, in force almost continuously since 1967, individuals can be detained without charge or trial on exceedingly broad security grounds, which had led to the institutionalization of arbitrary arrest and detention by security forces.

As in some other countries where the same agency deals with individuals both at the police (investigative) stage and at the convictions (punitive) stage, custodial confinement in Egypt is particularly abusive. That is, precisely because the Ministry of Interior has systematically violated the human rights of security detainees, it cannot be expected to safeguard the rights of inmates—security and criminal alike—in thirty prisons throughout the country. The situation merely is exacerbated by the weak—often nonexistent—oversight of the prisons by the Ministry of Justice and the Prosecutor General's office, and by the government's lack of receptivity to monitoring of the penal system on an ongoing basis by Egyptian nongovernmental organizations.

When confronted with criticism regarding prison conditions, governments invariably cite budgetary constraints. But various appalling conditions and practices in Egypt's prisons are irrelevant to that explanation and could be remedied with changes of policy alone:

● Egyptian prisons are incredibly filthy, a problem that could be solved by employing idle inmates in maintenance.

● Incoming security detainees are often subjected to particularly punishing conditions—including long periods of confinement inside their

---

[2]These abuses are documented in Middle East Watch, *Behind Closed Doors: Torture and Detention in Egypt* (Human Rights Watch, New York: July 1992).

cells, sometimes for months—for no apparent reason other than their status as actual or perceived members of anti-government political groups.

● Unsentenced security detainees are removed from prison to the custody of State Security Investigation, sometimes for torture, and then taken back to prison, without recording the transfers in prison records (see Chapter One), due to collusion between the Prisons Administration and State Security Investigation—the elite internal-security branch of the Ministry of Interior.

● Inmates can be whipped—or beaten, if they are juveniles—as an authorized disciplinary measure, despite Egypt's ratification of the International Covenant on Civil and Political Rights, which prohibits "torture" or "cruel, inhuman or degrading treatment or punishment" and requires that "all persons deprived of their liberty shall be treated with humanity and with respect for the inherent dignity of the human person"; and the Convention against Torture and Other Cruel, Inhuman or Degrading Treatment or Punishment, which requires states to ensure that acts of torture (defined as the intentional infliction of "severe pain or suffering") are made crimes under its laws and that offenders are prosecuted and punished.

● The existing serious overcrowding is sometimes deliberately exacerbated by the uneven distribution of inmates within prisons. In some of the most overcrowded institutions, entire cells remain empty.

● Inadequate light and ventilation similarly is made worse by the deliberate bricking-in of windows and, in two major facilities, the construction of cinderblock walls in front of cells where inmates are held for long hours daily.

Eliminating these problems simply requires an act of will by the authorities, not an increase in the prison system's budget.

The overwhelming majority of prisoners in Egypt's penal system suffer abuses silently. Most inmates are unaware of their rights, including the right to complain to representatives of the judicial branch of government, who are required to meet with prisoners on a monthly basis and take complaints. But because this system of so-called external oversight does not function properly, and because representatives of Egypt's independent legal and human-rights communities are barred from inspecting prisons and meeting with inmates in their cells, the only recourse that aggrieved prisoners have is to complain directly to the very prison authorities who carry out or condone abuses.

It is difficult to take at face value the reassurances given to Middle East Watch by government representatives, including the Prosecutor General, Chancellor Raga el-Araby, that abuses do not occur because an effective system to deal with complaints is in place. Our own four letters to the Prosecutor General sent since March 1992—in response to reports of serious abuses within prisons—have gone unanswered as of this writing.

This state of affairs leaves most prisoners unprotected, too afraid—or too skeptical—to speak out for fear of retribution. In rare cases, prisoners with legal support have challenged punitive and illegal practices in the courts and secured justice, but only after lengthy proceedings. It took a lawsuit by four sentenced prisoners in the maximum-security prison at Tora to secure a court ruling in January 1992 that their continuous solitary confinement was in violation of the law (see Chapter Four). The court also found that the denial of radios, newspapers and books to these prisoners violated the law.

The testimony of those prisoners who agreed to speak to us, combined with own our observations during prison inspections, left us with a firm conviction that immediate prison reform is an urgent necessity in Egypt.

CONCLUSIONS

The findings of this report, summarized below, are based on our observations at the prisons we inspected, information obtained from former and current prisoners, comments by prison commanders and other officials, and supplemental research.

PRISONERS' RIGHTS

The right of prisoners to humane treatment is set forth in the Egyptian Constitution and Egyptian law. In theory, mechanisms are in place to uphold this right and provide inmates with avenues to complain about mistreatment and other grievances. Under Egyptian law, prisoners have the right to complain to prison authorities who, in turn, must accept and record any complaint in the prison register and transmit it immediately to the *niyaba al-'amma*, an institution within the Ministry of Justice (see Glossary). These rights are not respected.

Further, literate inmates are not provided with written notice of a prison's rules and regulations upon arrival at the institution, a violation of international standards. Officials told us that prisoners are adequately informed orally about the grounds upon which they may be subject to punishment. This is no substitute for the provision of written rules and merely is an invitation to arbitrary punishment. As one inmate at Qanater men's prison wrote to us in October 1992: "We have reached a stage where we no longer know what is permitted or prohibited in this jail. One official will permit something and when another one comes, he will prohibit it. We do not know which one to follow."

OVERSIGHT OF THE PENAL SYSTEM

External oversight of the Prisons Administration is the responsibility of the niyaba within the Ministry of Justice. By law, representatives from the niyaba are required to undertake monthly, unannounced prison inspections in order to monitor prisoners' treatment. Among other duties, they should take complaints from prisoners about mistreatment.

6 ● CONCLUSIONS

Egypt's Prosecutor General, Chancellor Raga el-Araby, assured us that there is "complete supervision" of the prisons and that there are "periodic inspections." He said that niyaba inspections "take place at least once every month and immediately after any complaint." But we found that the overwhelming majority of inmates rarely if ever have access to an inspector from the niyaba during periodic prison visits. Virtually all male prisoners we interviewed insisted that they had never seen a niyaba representative on an inspection visit. In fact, most prisoners were astonished to learn from us that a niyaba representative was required to visit prisons on a monthly basis and take complaints. Former prisoners we interviewed noted that they, too, never saw a niyaba while they were incarcerated.

AUTHORIZED DISCIPLINARY MEASURES

Egyptian law authorizes the beating of juvenile prisoners and the whipping of adult prisoners as a disciplinary penalty. Both practices are proscribed by the Egyptian Constitution and are clear violations of international law. International rules for the treatment of prisoners also prohibit corporal punishment for disciplinary offenses.

Under Egyptian law, prisoners can be placed in solitary confinement for up to fifteen days for each disciplinary offense. Our inspections of punishment cells revealed appalling physical conditions, confirming one prisoner's description of these cells as "dirty rooms without anything." Not one of the many punishment cells we inspected had a toilet or running water, and most reeked with odors from the small metal cans that had to be used for sanitary purposes. Most cells were filthy and poorly lit, and had no mattresses, only several thin prison-issue blankets on the floor. We also found wide discrepancies in the amount of time that prisoners were permitted outside punishment cells on a daily basis, with the "break" ranging from five to thirty minutes.

UNAUTHORIZED PUNISHMENT

We discovered, in random inspections, punishment cells that were being used for unauthorized purposes. In a cell at Abu Za'bal Liman we found a young criminal inmate whom officials described as "crazy." He had been placed in the punishment cell the day before on orders of the prison doctor because he could not get along with his cellmates. In a punishment cell at Tanta prison, we found a teenage detainee who was placed there because he refused to confess to the criminal offense for which he was arrested. We randomly encountered three other prisoners who had been held in punishment cells beyond the legal limit of fifteen days' confinement, including a fifty-year-old Palestinian housewife, a security detainee, who told us that she was brought to her small cell upon arrival at the prison seventeen days earlier and that her door had never been unlocked.

UNAUTHORIZED PHYSICAL ABUSE

Although we found no evidence that torture or the most severe forms of physical abuse are used systematically within Egypt's prison system, we did meet many torture victims among the security prisoners held in Tora Istikbal and Abu Za'bal Liman prisons. As documented in a Middle East Watch report published in July 1992, security detainees as a matter of practice are tortured during interrogation by SSI prior to their transfer to prison, and sometimes are secretly removed from prisons to be tortured in SSI custody.

This conclusion does not mean that Egyptian prisons are free from physical abuse. We collected information about incidents from 1989 to 1992 in which male prisoners have been beaten and whipped. Most alarming about this physical violence is that some of it was premeditated and organized, carried out in the presence of prison officers. At least some of the beatings have been *highly* organized, involving large numbers of soldiers. We documented numerous instances of beating in prisons, including during cell searches and in retaliation for participation in a hunger strike to protest prison conditions. We received testimonies of the use of electric prods and leather whips with pieces of metal attached. In at least one case we received testimony about prisoners being made to walk through gauntlets of soldiers who beat them.

8 ● CONCLUSIONS

PUNISHING CONDITIONS FOR SECURITY DETAINEES AND SENTENCED PRISONERS

There is substantial evidence that prison officials impose particularly harsh living conditions on sentenced security prisoners and security detainees held without charge under the Emergency Law for either short or long terms. These conditions rise to the level of deliberate collective punishment. This policy appears to be long-standing at Tora Istikbal, where many security detainees have been and continue to be held.

In addition, particularly harsh disciplinary measures are often applied without these detainees or prisoners having committed any disciplinary infractions. In January 1992, an Egyptian court ruled that the authorities at Tora Liman prison violated the law by subjecting sentenced security prisoners to prolonged solitary confinement and denying them newspapers, books and other items.

UNRECORDED REMOVAL OF SECURITY PRISONERS FROM PRISONS

One of the most serious problems in the Egyptian prison system, which affects security detainees held without charge under the Emergency Law, is the temporary—and unrecorded—removal of detainees from Tora Istikbal and Abu Za'bal Liman prisons to State Security Investigation (SSI) offices in Cairo. Detainees typically are blindfolded and transported there at night. After a period of several days to one week, they are returned to prison.

Detainees are removed from the prisons for two reasons: for interrogation by SSI—sometimes accompanied by torture—in incommunicado detention, and to facilitate continuous long-term detention after their release by a court. The latter purpose allows the authorities to claim that detainees have been released pursuant to court orders, when in fact they have simply been temporarily "disappeared" at SSI offices. They are held in SSI custody until new detention orders can be written.

TREATMENT OF FOREIGN NATIONAL PRISONERS

Some of the most vulnerable inmates in Egypt's penal institutions are foreign prisoners, often men and women from other African countries, some of whom are serving lengthy sentences, including life imprisonment. Indigent foreign nationals endure particularly harsh living conditions because so little is supplied by the prison authorities. Unlike their Egyptian counterparts, most foreign nationals do not benefit from regular family visits and the receipt of needed items. Some "work" for Egyptian prisoners in exchange for food, clothing, prescription medicines and other items; other inmates beg for donations.

MEDICAL CARE AND FACILITIES

The most serious complaints we heard about medical care concerned the denial of medical attention to prisoners who urgently required treatment or who had been recommended for specialized care at outside hospitals. Security prisoners in particular appeared to have difficulty securing permission for treatment in outside hospitals.

Some prisoners mentioned the names of individuals who had died in prison hospitals or in their cells allegedly because of poor or nonexistent medical care, such as a prisoner in his sixties at Tora Mazraa prison, who had been thirty days from completion of a twenty-year sentence for a narcotics offense, and who died after being denied medical attention for three hours following an apparent heart attack.

We took complaints from prisoners who said that they were ill and had been denied requests to be examined by prison doctors. Other prisoners had been seen by the doctor but received only superficial examinations, or were provided only aspirin for various medical problems. Testimony indicated that at some prisons it was necessary to bribe staff to obtain admission to the hospital.

Inmates also told us that prison doctors only provided prescriptions for medication, and that they or their families had to purchase the medicine, placing life-threatening hardships on impoverished Egyptian and foreign prisoners.

10 ● CONCLUSIONS

Our inspections revealed that filth and poor sanitary conditions prevailed in hospital wards and bathrooms. In some wards, patients slept on filthy blankets and sheets. We saw wards that were severely overcrowded, with some prisoners in beds but others sleeping on thin blankets on the floor. Bathrooms for patients typically were extremely dirty and some toilets were inoperative or lacked running water.

LIVING CONDITIONS

Overcrowding is a major problem in Egyptian prisons, many of which were constructed in the late nineteenth century. While not all prisoners were held in overcrowded cells, we saw many cells that were severely overcrowded, such as the 20-by-100 foot dormitory cell at Tora Liman prison that housed 147 men, and the 10-by-20 foot cells in Tanta prison that were packed with twenty-five or more inmates. We found that overcrowding was not simply the result of prisons being filled beyond their capacity but rather, in certain facilities, quite deliberate. At some prisons, terribly overcrowded cell conditions existed while—doors away or a floor above—cells were empty, some of them showing evidence of having been empty for quite some time.

Sanitary Facilities and Water Supply: Sanitary conditions were in blatant violation of international standards. Inside many cells, there were no toilet facilities or running water. Prisoners in these cells had limited access to outside toilet facilities, and were forced to use buckets for toilets and bottles of water for drinking and personal hygiene. Toilets that we saw sometimes were inoperative. Where there were in-cell facilities, they simply were inadequate for the number of inmates forced to share them—in the extremely crowded dormitory cell at Tora Liman, for example, there were only three toilets for 147 men.

At several prisons, inmates complained that the water ran irregularly and then only for short intervals. Some security prisoners suggested that the water supply was cut as a means of punishment. Current and former prisoners complained about the contamination of drinking water at the three-prison Abu Za'bal complex. We observed visibly dirty water running from the faucets in two washrooms at Abu Za'bal Liman. This serious problem has persisted at least since 1989.

Light and Ventilation: Prisoners live in cells with inadequate light and poor ventilation. Prison authorities have taken actions which exacerbate these problems and deliberately create punishing conditions. We found some cells in which the windows had been partially bricked in and the small windows on the doors covered up. Cinderblock walls had been constructed in front of the cells on the first floors of two of the prisons visited. These walls effectively blocked the cells from the ventilation and light provided by spacious atrium courtyards.

Sleeping Accommodations: At most Egyptian prisons, beds are not supplied for inmates. The vast majority of prisoners in the prisons we inspected slept on mattresses, mats or blankets on stone or cement floors. In attempts to fight the cold during the chilly winter months, some prisoners placed their mats or blankets on sheets of cardboard. According to prisoners, cardboard could be purchased from guards, but guards sometimes confiscated cardboard as punishment.

Food: Numerous inmates and former prisoners complained that prison food was of poor quality and insufficient quantity. We saw that prisoners supplement their diet extensively with food supplied by their families, pool these supplies, and prepare collective meals.

Indigent prisoners from other countries, most typically Africans, who receive no food from the outside, are forced to beg for donations from other inmates or to work for wealthier prisoners as servants in exchange for food. In addition to this difficult situation for foreign nationals from poor families, another major consequence of the family-subsidized food-supply system is that inmates held in isolation during the first thirty days of their confinement, or those held in punishment cells, are reduced to a meager diet. The same problem is experienced by security detainees who are held for short periods and then released. During the first month of detention no family visits are allowed, forcing these detainees to rely solely on prison rations. The same situation prevails for other Egyptian prisoners whose families do not, or cannot, visit them on a regular basis.

12 ● CONCLUSIONS

TIME OUTSIDE CELLS

Officials stressed that inmates were allowed out of their cells for at least one hour daily. For most male prisoners in the facilities we visited, this policy appeared to be in effect. But for many prisoners, security and criminal alike, time *outside* their cells did not mean time *outdoors* in fresh air and sunlight. Cells simply were unlocked and inmates permitted to walk in interior atriums. Women prisoners, in contrast, complained that they were rarely let out of their extremely crowded dormitory cells. Such conditions are in flagrant violation of minimum international standards, which require at least one hour of exercise in the open air daily for *all* prisoners not engaged in outdoor work.

From prison to prison, and even within the same facility, we found considerable variation in the amount of time prisoners were allowed out of their cells on a daily basis. The most serious complaint about confinement came from security prisoners, who spent long hours locked inside their cells. Some security prisoners held without charge at Tora Istikbal told us that they had not been let out of their small, crowded cells for months at a time; others received a daily forty-five-minute break outside their cells but inside an atrium walkway—not outdoors.

This prolonged daily confinement was a major issue in the hunger strike that was in progress by the security detainees at Tora Istikbal when we visited that prison. We received many handwritten notes from striking prisoners, demanding a change in the confinement policy. "We request a break from 8:00 in the morning until 4:00 in the afternoon," several notes read. Other petitions demanded the "sun parade" in the prison yard. "The break is very short, and we don't see the sun," one detainee wrote.

WORK AND OTHER ACTIVITIES

Idleness is the predominant feature of daily life in Egyptian prisons. At each prison we visited, work opportunities for sentenced prisoners, both men and women, were extremely limited.

With few work opportunities and the terrible overcrowding, education and recreation programs become all the more important. But, according to the Prisons Administration's own statistics, a mere 0.4 percent of all prisoners are engaged in secondary education programs, and 0.7 percent in university study. The prisons we inspected had no organized physical and recreational training programs, with the exception of Tora Mazraa. At some facilities, physical recreation appeared to be limited to a very small number of hand-picked prisoners.

Prisoners are permitted to receive only three Egyptian daily newspapers, all of them part of Egypt's "semi-official" press. Opposition daily or weekly newspapers are not permitted. Books are allowed but, according to the director of the Prisons Administration, "political books are not forbidden—but they are controlled." Newspapers and books are sometimes denied to security prisoners as a form of punishment. Four prisoners at Tora Liman mounted a legal challenge to the prison's discriminatory policy that had denied them books and newspapers. In a January 1992 decision, the court ruled that this practice violated Egyptian law and prison regulations. The court also ruled that the denial of radios to the prisoners at Tora Liman was unjustifiable and in violation of the law.

CONTACT WITH OUTSIDERS

With the exception of a "quarantine" policy that prohibits family visits for the first thirty days of detention—and sometimes longer for security prisoners—the authorities generally are in compliance with international standards which mandate that prisoners receive visits from family and friends at regular intervals.

Most of the complaints that we received centered on the thirty-day "quarantine" and on the time allowed for a visit, which inmates said was too short. We learned that the length of time allowed for family visits varies from institution to institution and—sometimes—from prisoner to prisoner. They ranged from ten minutes to half an hour.

Islamist prisoners at Tora Liman and Tora Istikbal complained about the treatment of their families by prison officials during visits, including insults by prison personnel and forcing families to wait in the sun for up to five hours before they are allowed into the visitors' room. Detainees also complained about cumbersome visit-authorization procedures, which require families to first visit an office in downtown Cairo before going to the prison, placing an additional hardship on relatives coming from afar.

WOMEN PRISONERS

In conformity with international standards, women prisoners in Egypt are held in separate women's sections at general or central prisons, or in the large women's prison at Qanater. We found that in one important respect—long periods of daily confinement inside their cells—women inmates at Qanater are treated more harshly than most male prisoners.

At both Qanater prison and the women's jail at Tanta prison, women complained about overcrowded, poorly ventilated cells and the oppressive heat during the summer months, particularly troublesome during the times they were confined to their cells. We found the cells at Qanater visibly cleaner than those in other prisons, but inmates indicated that this was due to a deliberate clean-up by prison officials, prior to our visit.

Women are allowed to bring infant children with them to prison, and inmates who give birth in prison are allowed to keep their babies until the children reach two years of age. Upon reaching the age of two, children are given to the inmate's family if they wish to take them; otherwise, they are placed in an orphanage.

We found a wide disparity at Qanater and Tanta between the arrangements for prisoners with children. While Qanater has a nursery, at Tanta infants and their mothers were packed into the same overcrowded cells as other prisoners, and slept in less than ten square feet each on dirty cement floors.

We found that work opportunities for sentenced women prisoners were also extremely limited. At Qanater, there were only three workshops, employing forty-three of the prison's 1,100 women—less than four percent, lower than the already-low rates for male prisoners. We saw no recreational facilities for women at Tanta or Qanater.

The prison mosque at Tanta is off-limits to women prisoners. Four women sharing a cell, all of them religious Muslims, told us that they prayed in their cell: "The mosque is only for the men."

RECOMMENDATIONS

Middle East Watch offers the following recommendations for consideration by the President of the Republic, the Minister of Justice, the Prosecutor General, the Minister of Interior, and the Director of the Prisons Administration:

1. Take immediate measures to ensure independent and meaningful oversight of the treatment of inmates throughout the penal system.

The overwhelming majority of prisoners who suffer grievances clearly lack access to outsiders who are independent of the Prisons Administration and with whom complaints can be registered, as required by Egyptian law. One remedy is to open up the prison system, and permit ongoing monitoring by Egyptian nongovernmental human rights groups, professional organizations of lawyers and medical doctors, and other qualified observers.

A parallel remedy is to improve the mandated oversight role of the Ministry of Justice. The system of niyaba inspections must be overhauled to ensure that prisoners and detainees actually *see* niyaba representatives during their monthly visits and thus have an opportunity to speak with them about grievances and to report gross abuses. One confidence-building measure that should be considered is to allow independent monitors (from lawyers' and human rights groups, for example) to accompany the niyaba and observe that sections of each prison are visited, that complaints are taken, and that follow-up actually takes place.

While MEW applauds the Egyptian government for opening its prisons to the scrutiny of an international human rights organization, we caution that for access to be meaningful, it must be ongoing and extended to local human rights monitors. Local monitors are better situated and best equipped to inspect prisons regularly and undertake advocacy on behalf of aggrieved inmates.

MEW further recommends that the Egyptian government invite the International Committee of the Red Cross (ICRC), which already carries out various program activities in Egypt, to visit security prisoners and detainees on an ongoing basis and to provide them with humanitarian services. By providing such access to the ICRC, which performs this function in many other countries around the world, the Egyptian government would be assured of accurate yet strictly confidential information about prisoner treatment.

2. Instruct all prison commanders to provide written information to all prisoners—those already incarcerated and all incoming inmates—about disciplinary rules and prisoners' rights, and in addition establish a parallel system of information for illiterate prisoners.

In compliance with international standards, upon admission to a prison all literate prisoners should be provided with a copy of the institution's rules and disciplinary procedures, including the procedures used for the redress of grievances. In addition, the oversight role and functions of the niyaba should be explained in writing. Detailed oral instructions should be provided to illiterate prisoners.

3. Eliminate beating and whipping as forms of authorized corporal punishment.

The use of beating and whipping as authorized punishment, or any other form of corporal punishment, should immediately cease, in compliance with the requirements of the Egyptian Constitution and international human-rights treaties to which Egypt is a state party.

4. Investigate and vigorously prosecute all incidents of unauthorized punishment of inmates by prison officers and guards.

Unauthorized punishment, including physical abuse, must immediately cease. The niyaba on a monthly basis should inspect all punishment cells and meet with inmates held there to ensure that their treatment is in compliance with the regulations. Reported incidents of unauthorized punishment should be investigated by the Prosecutor General in a timely fashion, and those found responsible should be held accountable and prosecuted. Prisoners who provide information about abuses must be protected from retaliatory actions or additional punishment by prison officials—a situation that can, in large part, be prevented by regular monitoring of the prisons by representatives of independent organizations.

5. Investigate and cease the practice of unrecorded temporary removal of security detainees from prisons and into the custody of State Security Investigation (SSI).

The practice of the unrecorded removal of detainees from prisons to State Security Investigation (SSI) offices must end immediately. The problem has not been addressed by those responsible for internal and external oversight of the prison system. It merits urgent attention at the highest levels of the Egyptian government.

The Prosecutor General should investigate this practice, with a particular focus on its use at Tora Istikbal and Abu Za'bal Liman prisons. The Prosecutor General should examine individual cases in which detainees have been tortured while in SSI custody after their removal from prisons where they were registered. Responsible officials found complicit in these abuses should be prosecuted to the fullest extent of the law as required by the Convention Against Torture and Other Cruel, Inhuman or Degrading Treatment or Punishment, to which Egypt is a state party.

6. Investigate and ameliorate the particularly harsh and discriminatory treatment of security detainees.

7. Take immediate steps to investigate and correct deficiencies in the provision of medical care and treatment to prisoners.

Medicines should be supplied free of charge to all prisoners who are in need of medication. In no case should prisoners be required to purchase medicine with their own funds or to rely on families to bring drugs prescribed by prison doctors. Allegations that this is common practice should be investigated by the proper authorities; Prison Administration medical personnel found guilty of these practices should be disciplined.

A high-level working group from the Ministry of Health should be designated to conduct an independent and thorough inspection of the health care system and all medical facilities in Egyptian prisons as a matter of utmost urgency. In addition, an independent team of Egyptian doctors should be permitted access to the prisons, for the purpose of documenting specific problems (particularly with regard to sanitation and hygiene), and identifying actions that must be taken to remedy the situation and improve the conditions under which ill prisoners are being held.

The Ministry of Health must also investigate immediately the water quality at the Abu Za'bal prison complex, which prisoners complain has been contaminated since at least 1989.

8. Overcrowding must be reduced.

In addition to the construction of new prison spaces, the Prisons Administration should immediately implement a more even distribution of inmates within the existing spaces. It is unacceptable that prisoners are confined to terribly overcrowded cells while a large number of cells in the same wing remain completely empty.

While MEW welcomes all attempts by the Egyptian authorities to relieve overcrowding and improve living conditions for prisoners, the conversion of workplaces to living quarters—as discussed by the director of the Prisons Administration—will only exacerbate the serious problem of prisoner idleness.

9. The time prisoners spend each day locked in their cells should be decreased.

Every prisoner, including unsentenced security prisoners, should be allowed at least one hour of outdoor exercise daily. Efforts should be made to leave cells unlocked for several hours during the day, leaving prisoners free to move within their ward or building.

10. A serious effort should be made to provide inmates with work.

A desperate need exists for an expansion of meaningful work and employment opportunities. Prisoners could, and should be employed in the maintenance of the institutions. Filth in cells, bathrooms and hospital wards can be eliminated through regular maintenance work by the large number of prisoners who sit idle for years in airless, dimly lit cells. The assignment of such tasks would also provide daily relief from their terribly overcrowded living quarters.

11. The thirty-day "quarantine" period following inmates' arrival at a prison, when family visits are not permitted, should be abolished.

The lack of family visits during the initial thirty days in prison creates not only psychological but physical suffering for inmates. Given the fact that most inmates rely on relatives for their most basic necessities, such as food and medicines, the initial thirty-day period becomes the time when they have to endure the greatest hardship.

12. The length of family visits should be increased.

Visits of between ten and thirty minutes are too short. This policy is a particular hardship for family members who must travel from great distances to see their relatives. The authorities should implement a policy of allowing at least one-hour visits to all prisoners.

13. Create appropriate conditions for mothers and infants.

Under no circumstances should new mothers and infants be held in overcrowded cells without beds and access to running water.

14. All women prisoners who wish to pray in prison mosques or other religious institutions should be permitted to do so with the same frequency as male inmates.

1
EGYPT'S PRISON SYSTEM: AN OVERVIEW

In October 1975 as President I took up a pickax to strike the first blow at the wall of Turah Prison (thereby beginning its demolition)....The bricks were sodden and easy to break. Even the outer coat of plaster was obviously wet, and, as I removed it, innumerable cockroaches came out—ugly contingents of cockroaches. I still raised my pickax and hit at the wall, determined and tense, as though I could demolish it all myself....It was a memorable moment, for I was dominated by the feeling that such prisons should be removed and replaced by others fit for human beings.

— Anwar el-Sadat, writing in his 1977 autobiography, **In Search of Identity**.

In February 1992, Egypt's thirty prisons held 35,392 inmates, of whom 1,441 (four percent) were women. In a population of some fifty-seven million, this amounts to a ratio of approximately sixty-two prisoners per 100,000 population.[1] The capacity of Egyptian prisons is estimated at about 20,000.[2] Egyptian officials themselves readily acknowledge that the prisons are filled beyond capacity.

Over one-third of Egypt's prisons are concentrated in the greater Cairo metropolitan area, including the massive six-prison complex in Tora, a town southeast of Cairo; three prisons in Abu Za'bal, northeast of Cairo; and the men's and women's prisons in Qanater, northwest of

---

[1] Other incarceration rates per 100,000 population, based on 1990 or 1991 data, include: United States, 455; South Africa, 311; Venezuela, 177; Canada, 111; Australia, 79; Denmark, 71; Japan, 42; and India, 34. (Marc Mauer, "Americans Behind Bars: One Year Later," The Sentencing Project, Washington, D.C.: February 1992, p. 5.)

[2] As of the mid-1980's, Egypt's thirty prisons had a capacity of "fewer than 20,000 prisoners" but housed "about 30,000," according to a U.S.government-published study (Helen Chapin Metz, Ed. *Egypt: A Country Study*, Federal Research Division of the Library of Congress, Country Studies-Area Handbook Program sponsored by the Department of the Army, Fifth Edition: 1991, p. 347.)

Cairo. MEW visited sections in each of these three facilities, including Qanater women's prison.

Egypt's penal institutions are administered by the Prisons Administration, a department within the Ministry of Interior. At the time of MEW's visit, the Prisons Administration was directed by Gen. Mahmoud Fakarani, who said he reported directly to the Minister of Interior, Gen. Muhammad Abdel Halim Moussa.[3] Each individual prison is commanded by a Prisons Administration officer; multi-prison facilities have one overall commander with responsibility for the entire institution, and individual commanders who direct each separate prison within the complex. The staffs at Egyptian prisons include civilian employees of the Prisons Administration—described by officials as "government workers" who perform clerical and other functions—as well as guards and officers of various ranks.

CATEGORIES OF PRISONERS

The inmate population includes sentenced prisoners, prisoners under investigation, prisoners charged with offenses and awaiting trial or in trial proceedings, and detainees held without charge pursuant to Egypt's long-standing Emergency Law.[4] The prison authorities appear to keep prisoners strictly segregated by categories. Prisoners serving sentences for criminal and security offenses were housed in separate sections of a facility, and not mixed with unsentenced prisoners. Security prisoners in short-term (several months) and long-term (several years)

---

[3] In Egypt, Ministry of Interior officials and employees, including the various police forces, hold military-style ranks but are functionally separate from the army.

[4] Emergency law has been imposed continuously in Egypt since June 1967, except between May 1980 and October 1981. In May 1991, emergency law was extended for three more years. Under the emergency law, individuals can be detained without charge or trial on exceedingly broad grounds: suspicion of endangering public order or security. One legacy of long-term exceptional law in Egypt has been the institutionalization of arbitrary arrest and detention powers by security forces.

detention without charge or trial were also strictly segregated from other prisoners. Sentenced prisoners serving time for criminal offenses were separated from those serving sentences for security offenses. Among sentenced prisoners, MEW found those convicted of the same offenses—such as narcotics possession, or murder—were held together.

At the time of MEW's visit, as of February 19, 1992, officials said that there were 584 unsentenced security detainees in the prison system. The exact number of sentenced security prisoners is unknown to MEW, but it is low in comparison with those unsentenced.[5]

TYPES OF PRISONS

Egypt's prisons include general and central prisons serving specific geographic areas, special-purpose prisons (such as one reserved exclusively for draft-dodgers), and light-security to maximum-security institutions.

General prisons may serve one or several provinces, known in Egypt as governorates.[6] These facilities hold prisoners sentenced to a prison term,[7] prisoners sentenced to hard labor who have been

---

[5]The statistic reporting the number of unsentenced security prisoners provides an incomplete count of the total number of security detainees in Egypt on any given day. The daily statistics compiled by the Prisons Administration include only those detainees who have been admitted to a prison; omitted are security detainees who typically are first held incommunicado, for days and sometimes for over one week, at offices of State Security Investigation (the department within the Ministry of Interior responsible for internal-security matters in Egypt) or at military camps of the Central Security Forces, the 300,000-strong paramilitary force attached to the Ministry of Interior. For additional information, see *Behind Closed Doors*.

[6]For example, Tanta General Prison serves the governorates of al-Gharbiyah and Kufr al-Shaykh, according to the prison's commander.

[7]A "prison term" as defined in Article 16 of Egypt's Penal Code, is a sentence of not less than three years or more than fifteen, except in special cases specified by law.

transferred from a maximum-security prison, prisoners sentenced to a jail term of more than three months,[8] and women sentenced to hard labor. Central prisons hold prisoners sentenced to a jail term of less than three months (or with less than three months remaining when sentenced), prisoners subject to coercive detention to enforce a judgment of a pecuniary penalty, and persons detained pending investigation.[9]

There are three maximum-security prisons in Egypt, which are known as *liman* prisons: Tora Liman, Abu Za'bal Liman and Wadi Natroun Liman. These facilities hold prisoners sentenced to hard labor for the most serious crimes.[10] The commander of the Tora prison complex told MEW that Tora Liman was "the most secure and heavily guarded" prison because "the most important political prisoners are there." MEW inspected both Tora Liman and Abu Za'bal Liman, and interviewed both criminal and security prisoners held in these facilities.

---

[8]A "jail term" is defined in Article 18 of the Penal Code as not less than twenty-four hours or more than three years, except in special cases specified by law.

[9]Prisoners held pending investigation may be held in general prisons. New mothers and pregnant women in the sixth or later month are always held at general prisons pending investigation.

[10]Hard labor is defined in Article 14 of the Penal Code as: "Sentencing the convict to the hardest labor as specified by the government, for the duration of his natural life if his prison sentence is for life; otherwise, for the duration of his prison sentence. A sentence of hard labor for less than life shall not be less than three years or more than fifteen, except in special cases specified by law."

The term "hard labor" is misleading. One senior Prisons Administration official told MEW that, historically in Egypt, hard labor meant precisely that: "Prisoners were sent to the mountains to quarry blocks of stone. The purpose was to torture people. Their legs were kept in iron shackles. In 1960, the Interior Minister decreed that this hard labor system be stopped, and that prisoners instead work in factories in liman prisons. Since this time, hard labor has had no meaning. The only difference is in the family-visit system. Sentenced prisoners receive visits every twenty-one days, but those sentenced to hard labor receive visits once a month."

Prisoners sentenced to hard labor must serve part of their sentences at a liman. They may be transferred to general prisons for three reasons: after they have served the lesser of three years or one-half of their sentence on good behavior; for health purposes; or when they reach sixty years of age.[11] The director of Qanater Prison told MEW that prisoners sentenced to hard labor pass some of their sentence (either one-half or three years, whichever is shorter) at a liman and then they are transferred to a general prison. He added, however, that a lapse in good behavior can result in prisoners being sent back to a liman.[12] Prisoners clearly seek to minimize the time they spend at a liman, where conditions are rigorous. As one prison commander frankly remarked to MEW: "General prisons are more comfortable than liman prisons."

Light-security facilities in Egypt include agricultural prisons. MEW inspected Tora Mazraa, which was built by the British in 1908. Officials described it as a general agricultural prison, which held 738 sentenced prisoners, including forty-five Egyptians and one American serving sentences for espionage.[13] Tora Mazraa was the least

---

[11]Law 396 of 1956 on prison regulations, cited in Abdallah Khalil and Amir Salem, *Prisons in Egypt*, Cairo: 1990, in Arabic.

[12]Other prison directors told MEW that transfer was available only after one-half or one-third of the hard-labor sentence was served with good behavior, suggesting some confusion at the individual prison level regarding the specific requirements for transfer of inmates to other facilities. Such confusion could explain repeated complaints of hard-labor prisoners that prison officials no longer transferred prisoners to lower-security jails.

[13]MEW representatives met with the prisoners convicted of espionage. They included twenty-eight Egyptians serving sentences for spying for Libya and seventeen Egyptians convicted of spying for Israel. Sammy Wassef, a U.S. citizen from Michigan and former medical student in Egypt, was convicted of spying for the United States in July 1989 by the Higher State Security Court (from which there is no formal appeal), and sentenced to ten years of hard labor. Although it is beyond the scope of this report, many of these prisoners complained about brief, unfair trials. In the case of Sammy Wassef, whose family has contacted the highest levels of the Bush Administration and the State Department to seek help to secure his release on humanitarian grounds, he was forced to sign a lengthy confession, written in Arabic, a language that he was unable to read.

overcrowded facility that MEW visited and had by far the best physical conditions.

In addition to the types of prisons described above, prison officials say that Egypt also has an *istikbal*, or reception, prison, one of the six prisons in the complex at Tora. Gen. Fakarani of the Prisons Administration explained to MEW that the prison's two atrium-style, four-story buildings, contructed in the early 1980's "were built not to be a prison, but to receive prisoners and hold them until they are sent to other prisons."[14] But MEW found that Tora Istikbal has, for all practical purposes, been converted into a long-term holding facility for security prisoners held without charge under the Emergency Law. When MEW visited this prison, it held 1,093 inmates, of whom 693 were criminal prisoners; the balance of the inmates were suspected radical Islamists, some of whom had been held there without charge for over three years.[15]

DEMOLITION AND CONSTRUCTION

In meetings with MEW representatives, Egyptian officials readily acknowledged that most of the country's prisons are old and overcrowded. Many of these institutions—at Tora, Assyut, Alexandria and Qanater—were built around the 1890's during the British occupation, according to Gen. Mahmoud Fakarani. Of the prisons MEW inspected, only Tora Istikbal was of recent construction. With the additional exception of the First Department at Abu Za'bal, the other facilities were at least fifty years old. Most, in fact, were built in the late nineteeth century. None of the prisons showed signs of adequate upkeep or major recent renovation.

A Prisons Administration document provided to MEW by officials stated that Egypt's prisons were filled over their capacity, and that plans were under way to address the problem: "Due to current major overcrowding of prisons with inmates that exceed the absorption capacity,

---

[14]MEW interview, Cairo, February 20, 1992.

[15]For additional information about these detainees, see *Behind Closed Doors*, pp. 155-160.

the Prisons Administration has enacted a plan for renovation and replacement approved by the Interior Ministry."

Officials told MEW that demolition of old prisons had begun and the construction of new facilities was budgeted. In 1990, the government demolished a hundred-year-old prison with a 1,000-inmate capacity in Beni Suef, a town seventy miles south of Cairo, and sold the land in order to raise money to finance the construction of new prisons. In Fayoum, also south of Cairo, an old prison with a capacity for 500 was in the process of being demolished at the time of MEW's mission; all prisoners had been removed from the facility as of January 1992.

Gen. Fakarani told MEW that a high-security prison will be built in the Tora prisons complex. At an estimated cost of LE 30 million (almost $10 million), the new prison will have a capacity for 1,000 inmates. Three additional prisons, each with a capacity of 2,500, will be constructed in Qata in the Giza district of metropolitan Cairo, in Fayoum, and in Damanhour, the capital of the large Nile Delta governorate of al-Buhayrah. Gen. Fakarani also indicated that several renovation projects will relieve some of the overcrowding, by converting prison workplaces—known as "factories"—into living areas. He noted, for example, that the soap factory at Tora Liman prison can be renovated to accommodate 700 inmates.

PRISONERS' RIGHTS

The right of prisoners to humane treatment is set forth in the Egyptian Constitution. Article 42 states: "Every citizen arrested, incarcerated, or having his freedom limited in any way must be treated in a way that maintains his human dignity and should not be harmed physically or mentally." Article 40 of the Law of Prisons similarly states that prisoners be treated with "human dignity" and without mental or physical harm.

Theoretically at least, mechanisms are in place to uphold these rights and provide inmates with avenues to complain about mistreatment and other grievances. Under Egyptian law, prisoners have the right to complain to prison authorities who, in turn, must accept and record any complaint in the prison register and transmit it immediately to the *niyaba al-'amma,* an institution within the Ministry of Justice (see Glossary for a description).[16] But MEW found that the systems of "internal" oversight by the Prisons Administration, and "external" oversight by the niyaba are not responsive to prisoners' complaints about treatment.

OVERSIGHT MECHANISMS

According to prison officials, internal oversight of the system is carried out by an internal investigation and security unit (*mabahith al-sijjin* in Arabic). Prison officials told MEW that each prison includes one or more internal-investigation officers who are responsible for investigating prisoners' complaints and enforcing prison rules and discipline on both guards and prisoners. These officers are supervised by a high-ranking officer in the Prisons Administration who directs the investigation unit, a position held at the time of MEW's mission by Gen. Mustafa Lutfi. Gen. Lufti told MEW that he was personally responsible for the investigation of complaints about prison conditions and claims of mistreatment, and that he reported directly to the director of the Prisons Administration.[17]

External oversight of prisons is the responsibility of the niyaba. Attorneys representing the niyaba are mandated to inspect prisons on a regular basis and, among other duties, to take complaints from prisoners about mistreatment. By law, the niyaba is required to undertake monthly, unannounced prison inspections in order to monitor prisoners' treatment.[18] The mandate for niyaba inspections is wide-ranging and includes monitoring of the following: valid legal grounds for incarceration; treatment of prisoners, including segregation of prisoners

---

[16]Article 43 of the Code of Criminal Procedure.

[17]MEW interview, Tora Liman Prison, February 13, 1992.

[18]Law 396 of 1956 on prison regulations, and Article 1747 of the guidelines for the niyaba al-'amma, cited in Egyptian Organization for Human Rights [EOHR], "Prisons in Egypt: The Model of the Tora District Prisons," August 1991, pp. 2-6, and Amnesty International, "Egypt: Arbitrary Detention and Torture Under Emergency Powers," May 1989, AI Index: MDE 12/01/89, p. 28.

by category; proper record-keeping; and proper implementation of court and niyaba orders.[19] In addition, Egyptian law grants any member of the niyaba and any president or vice-president of a court of first instance or appeal the right to visit prisoners within their areas of jurisdiction to check that no one is being held illegally, inspect prison registers, and contact any prisoners to hear complaints.[20]

Egypt's Prosecutor General, Chancellor Raga el-Araby, assured MEW that there is "complete supervision" of the prisons and that there are "periodic inspections." He said that niyaba inspections "take place at least once every month and immediately after any complaint." He noted that niyaba representatives should ask prisoners if there are any complaints about mistreatment, pointing out that under law prisoners have the right to complain to the niyaba and to have the complaint recorded. He noted that the niyaba is required to take down complaints that are made orally or those that are presented in writing by prisoners. In addition to the periodic visits, Chancellor el-Araby said that there is an immediate visit by a district niyaba if a complaint is received by the prosecutor general's office.[21] He added that any report by a niyaba representative must include prisoners' complaints.

"Therefore, any mistreatment of the prisoner inside the prison is impossible....If it does happen, you will find that the niyaba has investigated it. We look at these complaints firmly, in depth," he told MEW. Chancellor el-Araby said that he personally reviewed all niyaba prison-inspection reports and insisted that Egyptian prisoners are not mistreated: "I have been in office only six months and have received no complaints."[22]

---

[19]"Egypt: Arbitrary Detention and Torture Under Emergency Powers," p. 28.

[20]Article 42 of the Code of Criminal Procedure.

[21]The duty of the prosecutor to investigate complaints is found in Article 42 of the Criminal Procedure Code. "Egypt: Arbitrary Detention and Torture Under Emergency Powers," p. 28-30.

[22]MEW interview, Cairo, February 5, 1992.

Chancellor el-Araby's optimism regarding the efficacy of the niyaba system appeared to be directly contradicted by several testimonies collected by MEW (see below). In addition, on November 20, 1992, Middle East Watch sent a letter by facsimile to Chancellor el-Araby, requesting that his office initiate an investigation of a complaint received by Middle East Watch about the beating on September 6, 1992, of foreign nationals held in three cells at Qanater men's prison (see Chapter Four). We also asked for a copy of the results of the investigation. As of the date of the writing of this report, Middle East Watch had not received a reply from the prosecutor general.

PRISONERS' LACK OF ACCESS TO NIYABA INSPECTORS

MEW is unable to dispute the Prosecutor General's claim that he noted no prisoner complaints in niyaba inspection reports. But one reason for the lack of complaints clearly is that the overwhelming majority of inmates rarely if ever have access to an inspector from the niyaba during periodic prison visits.

Virtually all male prisoners interviewed by MEW insisted that they had never seen a niyaba representative on an inspection visit.[23] In interview after interview, MEW would ask prisoners when they last saw a lawyer from the niyaba. This question typically was met by blank stares of incomprehension, or a prisoner's patient explanation that he had been brought to the niyaba to be investigated before he was charged with an offense. Most prisoners were astonished to learn from MEW that a niyaba representative was required to visit prisons on a monthly basis and take complaints. For example, prison officials at Tanta Prison told MEW that the niyaba had conducted an inspection visit just ten days prior to MEW's visit. If the niyaba did in fact visit, he was not seen by the many prisoners and detainees interviewed by MEW, for example, six occupants of a cell in Building A, all of them under investigation for forgery. Two of the inmates had been held in the cell for four months and both of them said that they had never seen a niyaba.

---

[23] Women prisoners, in contrast, told MEW that they did have access to niyaba representatives on more or less a monthly basis.

Sentenced prisoners at the maximum-security prison at Abu Za'bal, interviewed randomly by MEW representatives during inspections of their cells, likewise were insistent that niyaba representatives were never made available to them. One prisoner, who was serving his fifth year in this prison, said he "never" had seen the niyaba. Another prisoner who had been at Abu Za'bal for five years also said there was "no niyaba." A third prisoner, asked by MEW when he last saw a niyaba, replied "never." He was immediately interrupted by a prison official standing nearby. The prisoner then changed his testimony and told MEW: "Fifteen days ago the niyaba came."

The lack of access to the niyaba also was mentioned by former security detainees interviewed by MEW. A physician who was detained at Abu Za'bal prison from August to November 1989 said "the niyaba never visited us."[24] A student from the medical faculty at Mansoura University, arrested in February 1991 for participating in an anti-war demonstration in Cairo, was held without charge at Abu Za'bal prison for seventy-two days. "I never saw a niyaba in the prison," he told MEW.[25] A clerk held at Tora Istikbal from August to December 1991 said that he never had an opportunity to meet with the niyaba.[26] A Cairo shopkeeper held without charge at Tora Istikbal from February 1991 to January 1992 "never" saw a niyaba on an inspection visit during the entire time he was held there.[27]

The niyaba also plays a role during prison emergencies, such as hunger strikes. During MEW's visit to Tora Istikbal prison, a hunger strike was in progress by Islamist security detainees held without charge. The prison director, Gen. Hakim, told MEW that after a twenty-four hour waiting period, three high-level niyaba officials came to the prison to make a report. "They asked detainees the reasons for the strike, took down their demands, and recorded the state of their living conditions."

---

[24]MEW interview, Mansoura, February 3, 1992.

[25]MEW interview, Mansoura, February 3, 1992.

[26]MEW interview, Alexandria, February 1, 1992.

[27]MEW interview, Cairo, February 2, 1992.

The niyaba also gives advice to the prisoners, according to Gen. Hakim.[28] The striking detainees confirmed to MEW that the niyaba representatives had visited the prison on February 13, 1992 to conduct an investigation, although MEW is aware of no findings by the Prosecutor General that any of the striking detainees' demands had merit.

LACK OF ACCESS BY LOCAL HUMAN RIGHTS MONITORS

The Egyptian government's decision to open up the prisons for MEW's inspection in February 1992 was a significant first step toward independent monitoring of the prison system. But for access to be meaningful, it must be ongoing, of the sort that the International Committee of the Red Cross (ICRC) undertakes with respect to security detainees and prisoners in other countries. It was clear from MEW's visits to six facilities that prisoners were completely unaccustomed to seeing outsiders. Some prisoners, in fact, were visibly shocked. Given this, prisoners' level of suspicion was generally quite high, and many were reluctant to talk. Some of those who did provide information expressed fear that there would be retribution from prison officials after MEW representatives left the prison. (MEW received no complaints from Egyptian rights monitors and lawyers about retribution against prisoners following our visits.) If regular, ongoing visits to prisons by independent outsiders were instituted, inmates at least could hope that any penalties they might face for speaking freely would be exposed and investigated in subsequent visits. The regularity of inspections would also provide a strong deterrent to prison officials against various types of abuse, such as punishing inmates who complain or provide information to independent outside monitors.

The best-positioned monitors to carry out prison inspections on a regular basis are representatives of the ICRC, which would furnish information confidentially to the Egyptian government and provide humanitarian services to security prisoners, and Egyptian nongovernmental organizations. The Egyptian Organization for Human Rights (EOHR), for example, has repeatedly sought permission from the authorities to carry out prison inspections. In February 1992, EOHR

---

[28]MEW interview, Tora Liman Prison, February 13, 1992.

noted that while a U.S.-based organization was being afforded unprecedented access to Egyptian prisons, EOHR's own requests to inspect prisons have met with no response from the authorities.[29]

UNRECORDED REMOVAL OF SECURITY DETAINEES FROM PRISONS: AN INVITATION TO TORTURE

One of the most serious problems in the Egyptian prison system, which affects security detainees held without charge pursuant to the Emergency Law, is the temporary—and unrecorded—removal of detainees, mostly from Tora Istikbal and Abu Za'bal Liman, to State Security Investigation (SSI) offices in Cairo. Middle East Watch has devoted an entire report to the issue of the torture of security detainees.[30] Thus, here we only describe briefly the practice of unrecorded removals of prisoners from prisons.

MEW found that detainees typically are blindfolded and transported at night and are not informed about where they are being taken. After a period of several days to one week or more, the detainees are returned to prison. Detainees are removed from prisons for two reasons: for interrogation by SSI—sometimes accompanied by torture—in incommunicado detention, and to facilitate the continuous long-term detention of security prisoners who were ordered released by a court. The latter purpose allows the authorities to claim that detainees have been released pursuant to court orders, when in fact they have simply been temporarily "disappeared" at SSI offices. They are held in SSI custody until new detention orders can be written.

Detainees thus are left vulnerable and defenseless, and many are tortured after they are removed from prison. One detainee, who had been held without charge at Abu Za'bal for fourteen months, said he was removed from the prison to SSI headquarters in Cairo eight times and

---

[29]EOHR, "The EOHR Campaign Against Torture: Significant Results and Indications, Statement No. 4," Cairo, February 15, 1992.

[30]See *Behind Closed Doors.*

tortured. During MEW's visit to the prison, he passed a handwritten note that included the following appeal:

> I demand to be brought to forensic medical doctors[31] to document the torture to which I am continuously exposed. They drag me from prison and I am not told where I am going to be tortured. Then I am returned to prison another time, without this being written in the prison log and without anyone's knowledge.

During MEW's brief inspection of Tora Istikbal, detainees complained about their removal from the prison for torture in SSI offices. One detainee, who had been held without charge since January 1991, provided MEW with a letter of protest and demands:

> I have received eight releases from the court. After each release, I was transferred from Tora Istikbal to Lazoughly [SSI's headquarters in Cairo], where I was tortured. They renew my detention from Lazoughly and there I spend a period of ten to fifteen days. Following this, every time I have been transferred back to Tora Istikbal, where there is harassment and deprivation of my minimum rights as a political prisoner.

The detainee then provided a list of seventeen demands, including the recording of signs of torture on his body "in the book of the Prisons Administration upon my arrival back at the prison."

The problem of the unrecorded transfer of inmates from prisons into the custody of SSI has not been addressed by those responsible for internal and external oversight of the prison system. In fact, no prison official acknowledges this practice, which constitutes a breach of prison regulations.

---

[31]Some of the most incriminating evidence of torture of Egyptian detainees has come from forensic medical examinations conducted by Ministry of Justice physicians. See *Behind Closed Doors*, pp. 139-150, for information about the forensic medical reports prepared by these physicians.

Prison officials proudly told MEW that computerization of prisoner records began in 1989, and that computers have been installed at Tora, Abu Za'bal and Qanater prisons. Officials also noted that the computers at these facilities were in the process of being connected to the main Prisons Administration computer in Cairo. Officials pulled up a prisoner's file on the computer at Tora Liman prison for MEW, to demonstrate the information stored in the database. The file contained the following information: accusation; action taken; where action was taken (there were code numbers for various police stations); length of sentence; home address; date of birth; nationality; place of birth; education level; health status; previous arrests; release code; sex and marital status; behavior; and expected release date. Interestingly, the two prisons where unrecorded removals occur most often, Tora Istikbal and Abu Za'bal Liman, are among the first where the most efficient record-keeping methods have been put in place.

2
LIVING CONDITIONS

I was taken to cell 14....There was a hole in the floor to serve as a toilet and in one corner a pile of battered tin bowls....after only an hour the door of the cell was opened and a sergeant came in. 'Where's your bowl?' he asked brusquely. 'I haven't got a bowl," I said. 'There they are," he said, pointing to the pile in the corner. 'Take one for your food.' I saw that behind him was a soldier carrying a bucket full of horrible-looking molass and another soldier carrying a basket of bread covered in flies. 'I'm not going to eat that," I said....After a short while an officer came in. 'Why won't you take your food?' he asked. 'I know this is your first time in prison, but you'll have to get used to prison ways.'

> — *Mohamed Heikal, the prominent Egyptian journalist, describing his arrival at Tora prison following his September 1981 arrest in his book,* **Autumn of Fury (1983)**.

Prisons in Egypt are generally old and usually overcrowded. Prisoners suffer in cells with inadequate light, ventilation, and living space. Sanitary conditions generally are poor. And, as discussed in detail in the next chapter, many prisoners spend excessive periods continuously confined in their cells. In addition, MEW discovered that practices of the Prisons Administration deliberately exacerbate the severity of the conditions of confinement.

Prior to MEW's visits to the prisons, we had interviewed many former security detainees, who described abysmal conditions at the facilities where they had been held. The account that follows, from a university student who was held without charge at two different types of prisons from October to December 1991, typifies the complaints MEW heard. After inspecting Egypt's prisons, we found that this student's account, and the testimony of other former security prisoners, were accurate.

The student was first held at Assyut general prison after his arrest in October 1991. He was assigned to a cell with no toilet or running water inside. At times, the cell was occupied by three men. The room had no mattresses; the student and his fellow inmates slept on blankets. "Bad food" was provided once a day at noon, consisting of four flat round loaves of Arabic bread and some beans or lentils. The cell was unlocked only twice a day for inmates to use the toilets. Contact with the outside was sharply restricted: "In one month, I had no family visits and only one visit from my lawyer," the student said. After one month, he was transferred to Tora Istikbal prison.

> It was much worse. They cut my hair short and unevenly so it looked ugly. They took my clothes and gave me pajamas that didn't fit and were not warm enough for the winter weather. Clothes are not washed after they are taken from prisoners who leave. People get scabies and other dermatological diseases. You itch during the day and at night. You can't sleep.

The student was placed in a small cell on the ground floor. The door, which was locked shut at all times, had no window or peephole; the window inside the cell measured about three feet by eight inches.

> The toilet was a hole in the ground. I was given only one blanket, to use as a mattress and a cover. There was a high pipe in the cell, constantly dripping water. I spent a full month in this cell. There were no lawyer or family visits—it is forbidden during the first month. They never let me out of the cell. The door was opened only once a day, when they brought beans to eat. I had diarrhea and tonsillitis from the cold. I wanted to go to the clinic but I was refused. If you are ill, you knock on the door of your cell and the soldiers come and threaten to beat you. There was no electricity and no light at night inside the cell. If you are a student, you cannot study after dark.[1]

Detainees held for criminal offenses also suffer from poor living conditions. MEW interviewed an affluent Cairo physician and businessman in his late thirties who was arrested in October 1991, accused of bribery. While praising the conditions under which he was held

---

[1] MEW interview, Assyut, February 10, 1992.

at Tora Mazraa prison at the time of our interview, he bitterly described his first days of detention at two other prisons in Cairo:

> I was held on the second floor of el-Mahkoum Prison [Cairo Prison] for three days and two nights in an 8x5 meter room [about 26-by-16.5 feet]. There were forty men in the room which was locked from 4:00 pm to 8:00 am. We slept on thin mattresses. We didn't have sheets or blankets, but we didn't need them because it was still summer and the weather was hot.

He was then moved to Istinaf Prison. "I spent one day and two nights there. It was very bad...this must be the worst prison in Egypt," he said. "There was no mattress in the cell and just one blanket. There was no toilet, just a small pail. I was allowed outside the cell for only one hour a day. The toilets were so dirty I could not make myself even enter the room. There was no place to walk outside the cells. When they moved me to Tora Mazraa, I thought I was in paradise."[2]

Indigent foreign-national prisoners endure particularly harsh living conditions because so little is supplied by the prison authorities. Unlike their Egyptian counterparts, most foreign nationals do not benefit from regular family visits and the receipt of needed items. As one Asian prisoner serving a life sentence wrote in a letter to Middle East Watch: "We, as foreigners, have no money with which to buy new things, like a change of clothes or blankets or mattresses. We are not provided with any of these things. Only God can save us in the winter, when we have nothing to put on, and no blanket to cover us and protect us form the cold."[3] Another prisoner, an African, wrote: "Most of the foreigners from third world countries do not receive money from their parents and have to clean the rooms, toilets, clothes and sleeping places of the

---

[2]MEW interview, Tora Mazraa Prison, February 18, 1992.

[3]Undated letter, handwritten in Arabic, received by Middle East Watch on November 1, 1992 from an inmate in Qanater men's prison.

affluent inmates who reward them by providing them with food, clothing (prison uniforms), plates, stoves and pots, etc."[4]

OVERCROWDING

Overcrowding is a major problem in Egyptian prisons. While not all prisoners were held in overcrowded cells,[5] many cells inspected by MEW were severely overcrowded. The most severe overcrowding was best illustrated by the conditions in Cell Five in the criminal section of Tora Liman prison, one of Egypt's three maximum-security facilities.

Cell Five, a 20-by-100-foot dormitory, housed 147 men, providing about 13.6 square feet per person. The heat inside was overpowering from the overcrowding, despite the fact that the weather in mid-February was quite cool. When MEW representatives entered the cell, accompanied by prison officials, the inmates stood at attention, crowded shoulder to shoulder, and some of them saluted.

Once inside, one MEW representative dubbed the cell "The Boat" for its resemblance to the hold of an eighteenth-century slave ship. All available space in the dimly lit room literally was packed with men. There were no windows in the room, which reeked of spoiled food. The

---

[4]Letter dated October 28, 1992, from an inmate in Qanater men's prison.

[5]Overcrowding was not a severe problem at Tora Mazraa prison, for example. MEW found forty-four prisoners serving long sentences for political offenses housed in eight single cells and four 60-by-20-foot dormitory cells. Forty-eight prisoners convicted of espionage, also serving long sentences, shared four similar dormitory cells at Mazraa. Those in the dormitory buildings had beds spaced at regular intervals and, for the political prisoners, one cell was used as an informal mosque and library. The large dormitory cell of those convicted of espionage had several unoccupied beds. Both of these groups of prisoners at Mazraa benefited from the Egyptian government's adherence to a policy of keeping separate political and criminal inmates. Mazraa, however, is an exceptional prison in Egypt. Even the regular criminal inmates enjoyed a great degree of mobility within the prison and relative spaciousness inside their cells.

only light came from seven 4-by-6-foot steel grated skylights, which were partially covered by corrugated tin propped at an angle to keep out the winter chill. The fifteen-foot-high walls were covered from the floor to the highest point the inmates could reach with shelves packed with personal possessions in bags and boxes; other bags of possessions, including food, were hanging from nails in the walls.

The floor was almost completely covered with the mattresses, mats and blankets on which the inmates sat and slept. Placed perpendicular to the walls, the mattresses demarcated each prisoner's two-foot-wide living space. At the foot of each living space were pots and other containers, and heating elements used to prepare tea and cook the supplemental fresh and canned food brought to the prisoners by their families.

In the center of the room, between the two rows of mattresses, was an aisle formed by two raised brick curbs. Even in this six-foot-wide walkway, prisoners slept three or four abreast. While the semi-permanence of the other prisoners' mats, supplemented in many cases by six-inch-high string and cloth partitions, afforded a meager semblance of privacy, the prisoners who were forced to sleep in the aisle had their "privacy" further compromised. For inmates to reach the washroom at the rear of the room, the prisoners in the aisle had to take up their blankets. Moreover, those who slept in the aisle next to the washroom, in addition to enduring the smell of sewage and garbage emanating from the open flat toilets[6] and garbage cans inside, were forced to sleep on a dirty floor dampened by the muddy water that leaked from the dripping pipes, through the garbage and dirt, and down the several steps of the elevated washroom.

In Abu Za'bal Liman, another maximum-security prison, one convicted criminal prisoner interviewed by MEW in the vistors' area said

---

[6]"Flat toilets" are simple, flat fixtures, commonly made of porcelain, with a shallow depression and an open eight-inch wide hole in the middle. On either side of the hole are two pieces of raised porcelain or two inlaid bricks on which a person places his feet and stoops over the hole. The toilet is flushed by running water from a faucet, usually found above the toilet. In the prisons inspected by MEW, virtually all the toilets were of the flat type.

that he lived in Cell Two of the Third Department with 120 other sentenced prisoners. "There is no room in this cell," he said. "People are sleeping in the toilet area." Indeed, MEW found severely overcrowded conditions in this prison as well:

- In the Third Department, as many as seven inmates occupied small 6-by-12-foot cells, and twenty inmates were crowded into a 6-by-12-foot foyer area and a 4-by-100-foot hallway.

- In the First Department, MEW inspected a 15-by-25-foot cell with eleven inmates, and two 15-by-40-foot cells with thirty-six and forty-six inmates, respectively.

- A 15-by-30-foot cell in the prison's Fourth Department held forty inmates at the time of MEW's visit. A professor of medicine interviewed by MEW recalled that, when he was detained without charge in the Fourth Department from August to November 1989, the population of his 15-by-30-foot cell varied from forty to fifty inmates.[7]

At the general prison in Tanta, a city north of Cairo, MEW found 6-by-10-foot cells holding from five to seven inmates. Inmates in these cells, therefore, had only eight to twelve square feet of living space each. Larger 10-by-20-foot cells held twenty-five or more inmates, a mere eight square feet per person. In one cell in the women's jail at Tanta, thirty-nine women and four infant children were squeezed into a 300-square-foot cell, allowing only about 7.7 square feet per adult, without counting the infants.

At Qanater women's prison, most women slept in bunk-beds. In one 600-square-foot cell, each of sixty-two inmates had a bed, but in another 600-square-foot cell, seventy-three women shared forty-one bed spaces. As a result, over thirty women were forced to sleep between beds on the floor. In two other similar cells at Qanater, MEW found 105 and 107 women occupying seventy-one and sixty-nine beds, respectively. MEW also found fourteen women at Qanater cramped in a 150-square-foot cell with only one bed—little more than ten square feet per inmate.

---

[7]MEW interview, Mansoura, February 3, 1992.

In all of these overcrowded cells, the conditions for women resembled those of prisoners elsewhere in Egyptian prisons.

Deliberate Overcrowding

MEW found that overcrowding was not simply the result of prisons being packed beyond their capacity. In certain facilities, it was deliberate. At some prisons, terribly overcrowded cell conditions existed while—doors away or a floor above—cells were empty, some of them showing evidence of having been empty for quite some time.

At Tanta men's prison, at least nine cells on the second floor were empty, locked, and covered with dust. Several cells held only one inmate while, nearby, up to seven inmates occupied 6-by-10-foot cells and more than twenty-five inmates occupied 10-by-20-foot cells. Even more disturbing was the substantial number of empty cells in prisons where, doors away, inmates lived in less than twelve square feet of space each. For example, at Tora Istikbal as many as twelve inmates were held in 10-by-15-foot cells on the second, third and fourth floors, and up to seven inmates were held in 6-by-10-foot cells on the first and second floors. But MEW found during its inspection that fully one-half of the cells on the fourth floor, separated from the rest of the cells by barred gates, were *absolutely empty*. In all, fourteen 10-by-15-foot cells were empty. It appeared that no inmates had been held for some time in these dusty cells, to which the guards could not immediately find the keys. In addition to these empty cells, there were at least six other cells on the third and fourth floors that were completely empty, as well as several empty cells on the first and second floors.

Obviously, in order to carry out the Prisons Administration's stated policy of segregating security prisoners from criminal prisoners, and convicted prisoners from those under investigation or awaiting trial, some disparities in cell allocation might arise. This appeared to be the case at Tora Mazraa (where eleven security prisoners lived in cells that, across the prison, housed sixty criminal prisoners) as well as at Tora Liman. Assigning convicted murderers to single cells while other cells are overcrowded, as is the case at Tanta, is easily explained by security precautions. However, the prisoners MEW saw on the upper floors at

Tanta could not be distinguished in this manner. Government officials did not indicate any possible basis for this curious cell allocation.

The existence of these unutilized cells indicates that at some facilities overcrowding is a problem the Egyptian government has the ability to alleviate. MEW's discovery of such substantial numbers of empty cells in grossly overcrowded prisons is clear evidence that overcrowding, as it currently exists in Egyptian prisons, is not fully excused by the government's inadequate financial resources.

LIGHT AND VENTILATION

In addition to overcrowding, Egyptian prisoners endure confinement in dimly lit cells with inadequate ventilation and which are often dirty and damp. EOHR described conditions in Egyptian prisons in a 1989 report:

> Deteriorating prison conditions inside Egyptian prisons in recent years give serious cause for concern. In the punishment blocks...most vents have been completely sealed. [T]he detainee may be deprived of clean drinking water, and forbidden from using the lavatory. Often even the most basic hygiene standards are lacking. Cells may be infested with insects, have high levels of humidity, and be devoid of even the most basic facilities. The detainee may be prevented from moving throughout the day, and be forced to use the floor of his small and suffocating cell, where he spends the entire day, as a lavatory.[8]

MEW's inspections found that the problems described by EOHR three years ago continue in Egypt's prison system. In the sections that follow, specific aspects of the physical conditions at Egyptian prisons are examined.

---

[8]EOHR, "Torture in Egypt in 1989," January 11, 1990, p. 8.

Most cells visited were dimly lit. The cells in both nineteenth century and more recently constructed buildings have very small windows, placed at least six feet above the floor. Some cells have no windows at all, only skylights in the ceilings. These skylights, which usually measure 4-by-6-feet, could allow in lots of light. At the time of MEW's visit, however, most skylights were covered with wood, corrugated tin or plastic, presumably to keep out the winter chill. Most cells did have lightbulbs dangling from what appeared to be makeshift electrical wiring, which prisoners usually controlled.

Cell windows, which typically measure about 12-by-18-inches or smaller, open to the outside, allowing in light or sunlight for some portion of the day. Some cells also had small barred windows in or above the cell doors. The windows on the doors, however, were usually covered over with heavy steel plating. There were, in fact, very few cells with open door windows. The windows above doors usually did not allow much light into cells since they were typically ten or more feet above the floor and recessed in two-foot-thick walls.

The small, high windows also caused ventilation problems. Many cells MEW visited were hot, stuffy and smelly, despite the relatively cool winter temperatures in February.[9] Odors from dirty and sometimes inoperative toilets—or the open buckets used when cells lacked toilets—mixed with the smell of the tightly packed occupants and the heat generated by the electric lights and the cooking elements which many prisoners possessed to make the cells oppressive even in the winter. It is reasonable to assume that cell temperatures during the summer, when the outside temperature rises to ninety degrees Fahrenheit or higher, are oppressive.

While the problems caused by three factors—the climate, old prison buildings, and overcrowding—are serious enough, in many cases the prison authorities have taken actions which exacerbate these problems

---

[9]Throughout this report, it is important to remember that in Egypt the temperature becomes cool at night, even in the summer. Egyptian nights can be as cold as five degrees Celsius (about forty degrees Fahrenheit). As a result, a major concern for prisoners are blankets and clothing to keep warm, particularly during the winter.

and deliberately create punishing conditions. The construction of cinderblock walls in front of the cells, as is the case on the first floor of the First Department at Abu Za'bal Liman and the first floor of Building A at Tora Istikbal, is an example.

These walls block the cells from the ventilation and light provided by the spacious atrium courtyards. In the cells at Tora Istikbal, where 6-by-12-inch barred door windows would otherwise allow a cross breeze to ventilate the cells, the construction of the wall significantly reduced cell ventilation.[10]

Some cells had no windows at all. A thirty-four-year-old clerk, who was detained without charge at Tora Istikbal from August to December 1991, spent the first three months in a cell without windows. He told MEW:

> I was held in a cell with three others for three months. The window in this cell was completely bricked in. There was little ventilation and no light. I spent two months in complete darkness. We were not let outside the cell for two months.[11]

MEW found numerous cells in which the small barred windows on the doors had been covered up, and some regular cell windows that had been partially bricked in, reducing both ventilation and light, suggesting the deliberate creation of punishing conditions for those assigned to such cells.

---

[10]In a 1991 report, EOHR included the testimony of Talaat Fouad Quassem, an engineer held at Tora Istikbal, who noted that "the prison authority has constructed a high wall in front of the disciplinary wing to limit the sun and the air available to the wing's cells" in an apparent reference to Tora Istikbal's first-floor cells. EOHR, "Prisons in Egypt: The Model of the Tora District Prisons," August 1991, p. 18.

[11]This detainee was arrested on August 2, 1991, and held at a local police station until transferred to Tora Istikbal on August 8, 1991. MEW interview, Alexandria, February 1, 1992.

At least one group of sentenced prisoners at Tora Liman in the past had been denied artificial lighting in their cells. They told MEW that there were no electric lights "until last year. Then they began bringing us lightbulbs gradually, starting with those of us who were studying for [university] degrees."

SANITARY FACILITIES

MEW found sanitary facilities in blatant violation of international standards.[12] In many cases, there were no toilet facilities or running water inside the cells. Prisoners in many of these cells had limited or no access to toilet facilities and were forced to use buckets for toilets and bottles of water for drinking and personal hygiene. In some facilities, toilets and sinks were located inside cells, or in separate washroom facilities designed to serve the occupants of a number of cells.

When there were toilet facilities, MEW sometimes found them inoperative. In most cases where facilities existed, they simply were not adequate to serve the number of inmates forced to share them—such as the dormitory cell at Tora Liman that was packed with 147 men and contained only three toilets, or the cell at Abu Za'bal Liman where forty-six inmates shared two toilets. Garbage, raw sewage, and dirty water was found in both cells and washrooms. At no prison did MEW find that prison authorities provided soap or other hygienic supplies for the inmates.[13]

---

[12]Several provisions of the United Nations Minimum Rules discuss sanitary facilities. Article 12 requires adequate sanitary installations to enable every prisoner "to comply with the needs of nature *when necessary* and in a *clean and decent* manner." (Emphasis added.) Article 13 further requires that there be "adequate bathing and shower installations" to enable the prisoner to bathe "at a temperature suitable to the climate, as frequently as necessary for general hygiene...but at least once a week...." Article 14 requires that all areas of a prison normally used by prisoners be kept "scrupulously clean at all times."

[13]Article 15 of the Minimum Rules requires that inmates keep their persons clean and obliges the prison authority to provide them with water and "such toilet articles as are necessary for health and cleanliness."

The cells with the best sanitary conditions were the small cells, occupied by one inmate, that contained interior toilet facilities. In the cells at Tora Liman where convicted security prisoners were held, for example, each inmate occupied a small single cell with a flat-type toilet and an overhead pipe for a shower, located to one side of the cell behind a partition wall. It was at least feasible in these cells for the prisoner himself to keep the toilet area relatively clean. These small cells at Tora Liman, however, did have some problems. Poor ventilation forced the inmates to endure foul odors from the toilets. This problem was aggravated by the lack of running water during most of the day (see below).

At Tora Istikbal, in contrast, up to seven inmates occupied small, 10-by-6-foot cells, sharing the interior bathroom. Moreover, water ran through the prison's pipes, according to inmates, for only ten or fifteen minutes per day. Because of the lack of running water, prisoners stored water in buckets and bottles to use to flush the toilet, to wash, and to drink.

One prisoner wrote to MEW about the extremely limited access to toilet facilities when he was held at Tora Istikbal:

> There was no provision for defecation and urination. The cell is closed by 3:30 p.m. and opened at 8:30 a.m. The following morning when [the cell is] opened one is obliged to pay [the] equivalent of twenty cents before one is allowed to defecate and shower in the unhealthy lavatory situated within the detention premises.[14]

Inmates at Tanta prison expressed similar complaints. Some cells, holding as many as nine men, contained no sanitary facilities, except a small metal bucket to be used as a toilet when the men were confined to their cells from 11:30 am to 1:00 pm and from 4:00 pm to 8:00 am daily. "We absolutely cannot ask to use the washroom toilet when we are locked inside our cell," one prisoner told MEW.

---

[14]Letter to MEW, dated April 1, 1992.

Privacy in using toilet facilities is difficult if not impossible in overcrowded cells. Most cells only had partitions separating toilets from living area. In some dormitory-type cells, bathroom facilities are in a separate room, adjacent to the cell. But the extremely low ratio of toilets to inmates, the sporadic supply of running water, and the prevalence of diarrhea among inmates, leaves their condition extremely unsanitary.

The Cairo physician and businessman quoted at the beginning of this chapter described appalling sanitary conditions at el-Mahkoum Prison (Cairo Prison). He was held with forty other men in a 26-by-16.5-foot room that lacked an interior toilet:

> During the period the door was locked [from 4:00 p.m. to 8:00 a.m.], we were forced to urinate and defecate in a raised area in the cell, in front of the door. This area was about 1-by-1.5 meters [3.2-by- 4.9 feet]. There was no drain ... everything collected in this area until the morning, when it was removed by a sentenced prisoner.

At Tanta general prison, MEW representatives observed the yard that separated two four-story dormitory buildings filled with pools of sewage and standing stagnant water. This raised obvious concerns about the sanitary hazards for inmates occupying cells in close proximity to the percolating sewage.

WATER SUPPLY

In many prison cells—and even in hospital wards—water is stored by inmates in plastic one-liter bottles. At several prisons, inmates complained that the water ran irregularly and then only for short intervals. In one case, in a so-called tight-security cellblock at Tora Liman, MEW found that there was neither plumbing in the individual cells nor running water in the one washroom that served the section.

In one cell on the second floor of Tora Istikbal's Building A, some unsentenced security prisoners said that the water ran for only one to two hours a day. They showed MEW representatives the large plastic cans in which they stored water. Some prisoners at Tora Istikbal suggested that the water supply was cut as a means of punishment. An account provided by a trade unionist who was held at Tora after his arrest in August 1989 lends support to the allegations of current prisoners.

Mustafa Naib, a steel worker at the state-owned steel plant in Helwan, was detained from August 6, 1989 until November 25, 1989. He said that prisoners were punished by having their running water cut off for up to two weeks at a time, during which they were given small amounts of dirty lake water for drinking and washing. He said that the water was shut off twice while he was held at Tora. On one occasion, the cut-off was precipitated by the prisoners' refusal to accept bad bread, which led to a denial of their thirty minutes' exercise break. The prisoners then banged on their cell doors until security forces arrived and fired teargas bombs while the prisoners were confined to their cells.[15]

At Tora Liman, those accused of involvement in the 1990 assassination of Egyptian Parliament speaker Rifat al-Mahgoub were held in small cells that lack plumbing and thus running water. Outside there is a washroom with three toilets, a basin and three showers. There was no running water in this washroom, however, when MEW inspected it. The pipes, fitted with new spigots, were not connected to any main line, and there was no evidence that there had been any water, from any source, in the washroom for some time. In the whole section, in fact, MEW could find no water source.

The prisoners complained to MEW that until shortly before the February 1992 visit they had been continuously held in their cells. At the time of the visit, they said they were released in groups of five for about two hours daily, but still had no access to washing or toilet facilities. They attend to their personal hygiene in buckets in their cells, with water collected in bottles.

---

[15]Interview by Robert S. Lawrence, M.D., Cairo, May 26, 1990. Dr. Lawrence was a participant in a mission to Egypt in May 1990 as a representative of Physicians for Human Rights, the Boston-based organization. The other members of the delegation were Andrew Whitley, the executive director of Middle East Watch, and Arpiar Saunders, a penologist who travelled on behalf of the Prison Project of Human Rights Watch.

Drinking Water: Contamination at Abu Za'bal Prison

In addition to the problems noted above about the lack of a constant supply of running water at many facilities, we received numerous complaints from current and former prisoners about the contamination of drinking water at Abu Za'bal prison. Based on information MEW has obtained, this serious problem has persisted at the prison since at least 1989.

"The water was filthy and it made us sick. We got urinary tract infections and developed kidney problems," one former security prisoner told us. When members of the delegation inspected Abu Za'bal Liman, inmates in various sections of the prison complained about the quality of the drinking water supply. "The water has grit in it; it comes from the canal," said one sentenced prisoner who had been held in the same cell in the Fourth Department for ten years. "The water is dirty—we use tissues and rags to filter it. It comes from the canal," said a Palestinian administrative detainee held in the First Department. "The water makes us sick," another prisoner told MEW. "Our families bring us clean water."

On two occasions, in two different sections of the prison, inmates brought a MEW representative to the bathrooms at the rear of their cells. They turned on the faucet, placed a piece of clean white cloth at the top of the faucet, and let the water run through. The cloth quickly was stained with a reddish-brown color. The MEW representative asked for the piece of this cloth and placed it in a plastic bag. Months later, the cloth still retained its dirty tinge, and small pieces of dried, dark-colored particles were visible.

Engineer Kamil Khalil provided testimony about the poor quality of the water supply at Abu Za'bal in the summer of 1989. Khalil was transferred to the Industrial prison at Abu Za'bal in August 1989. He said that dirty water ran from a tap in his cell for only one hour daily, and that he and his cellmates filtered the water through cloth, which promptly turned brown, in an attempt to remove the most gross contamination.[16]

---

[16]Interview by Dr. Robert S. Lawrence, Cairo, May 26, 1990.

SLEEPING ACCOMMODATIONS

Most Egyptian prisons do not supply beds for inmates. The vast majority of prisoners in the prisons MEW inspected slept on mattresses or mats, or on blankets on the stone or cement floors of their cells.[17] Many prisoners complained about the dampness and cold of the floors, especially during the chilly winter months.

The sleeping accommodations for prisoners who sleep on the floor vary according to the prisoner's family's ability to supply bedding and other materials. Also, in an attempt to fight the damp cold of the floors, some prisoners placed their blankets on sheets of cardboard. According to prisoners at Tora Liman, inmates could purchase cardboard from guards. As a consequence, these prisoners alleged, guards sometimes confiscated cardboard as punishment.[18]

Only in Tora Mazraa and Qanater women's prison did most prisoners sleep on beds. However, some inmates at these prisons too were forced, like the inmates at all the other prisons MEW inspected, to sleep on the floor. In Qanater women's prison, MEW interviewed fourteen women who shared a 10-by-15-foot cell with a single bed. The women indicated that the bed was currently occupied by a pregnant cellmate. The thirteen others, all non-Egyptians, had no families to visit them and therefore each slept on the floor on a single blanket provided by the prison. The sleeping conditions were exacerbated by a large window that lacked glass, allowing in the winter cold.

---

[17]Some cells had tile floors, such as several cells at Tora Mazraa. Prisoners at Mazraa indicated that improvements such as floor tiles had been—and were required to be—financed by inmates themselves. In one of Mazraa's cells where prisoners convicted of espionage were held, one man explained that he and his cellmates had paid LE 300 (almost $300) to have tile installed in the cell's washroom.

[18]While MEW took few detailed testimonies about corruption in prisons, Egyptian prisoners and officials alike acknowledge it is a problem. In August 1988, then Minister of Interior Zaki Badr told a Cairo newspaper that "conditions inside prisons are terrible...the prisons are a hot bed of drug and monetary crimes...even more so among the guards themselves." *Egypt: A Country Study*, p. 348.

Women prisoners in the women's jail at Tanta did not have beds either. Twenty-seven and thirty-nine women slept on the floor in two 10-by-30-foot cells. Although there were seven women with children in the cell when MEW visited, there were no beds or other accommodations for the children at this prison (in contrast to the nursery cell at Qanater—see Chapter Eight). The infants slept with their mothers on the crowded, dirty cell floors, or were hung, hammock-like, in sheets from the walls.

Sleeping accommodations for prisoners that do not—or cannot—receive family visits are particularly harsh. The circumstances of a middle-aged Sudanese prisoner in a cell in the Fourth Department of Abu Za'bal are illustrative. This inmate, one of forty sharing the 15-by-30-foot cell, slept on the floor in front of the door to the cell's bathroom. He had no blankets, either from the prison or elsewhere and slept on three grain sacks.

The floor on which he slept, and from which he was protected only by the porous grain sacks, was damp and covered with muddy water that had dripped into the cell from the washroom. The door of the washroom was located at the head of what was this inmate's "bed." The stench of garbage and sewage inundated the area surrounding the washroom. The whole washroom was covered with algae and water. One of the Sudanese inmate's cellmates pointed out his condition and just shook his head: "We get nothing here; if you have no money, no nothing."

FOOD

There were no dining halls in any of the prisons MEW inspected. Prisoners eat in their cells on the floor, sometimes in the vicinity of toilets or the buckets used for sanitary purposes. Numerous inmates and former prisoners complained that prison food was of poor quality and insufficient quantity.

Food supplied by the prison authorities includes *foul* (a staple of the Egyptian diet, made from fava beans), lentils and rice, served in various combinations daily. Flat round loaves of Arabic bread, baked in prison ovens, are also supplied to prisoners each day; many prisoners and former prisoners interviewed by MEW said that four loaves were provided daily.[19]   Most inmates who complained about prison food nonetheless noted that prison bread was an exception and was good.

Officials told MEW that the vegetables grown on prison farms are consumed by the prisoners. Behind the mosque at Abu Za'bal Liman, MEW saw a garden with lettuce, onions and turnip greens in cultivation. (Officials said that the gardening was done by inmates with good behavior whose sentences were nearing completion.) On another occasion, MEW saw prison guards distributing fresh lettuce to prisoners at Tora Liman. Prisoners in one cell in Abu Za'bal Liman told MEW that earlier that day they were fed foul, lentils, cooked zucchini and radish greens. They also said that they received four loaves of bread daily and meat once a week.

One inmate of Qanater men's prison, serving a sentence of life imprisonment on a narcotics charge, wrote to Middle East Watch about the food supplied by the authorities there:

> All we get per day is some foul in the morning, and some
> rice and lentils for our main meal. The foul is very dirty
> and it is usually black in color. The rice is unwashed and
> unsifted, and there is a lot of dust in it. I have been here
> for five years and this horrible routine has not changed.

He added that every Monday prisoners received jam and cheese, and every Thursday a small piece of meat.[20]

Some former security prisoners also complained that food was supplied by the prison authorities only once a day and that it was of exceedingly poor quality. The student held at Assyut general prison for one month in October 1991 said that his daily diet consisted of four pieces of bread and some foul or lentils. A former member of Parliament who was held at Tora Istikbal in 1991 said he received four loaves of bread and one cup of foul in each twenty-four hour period. A teacher

---

[19]One Prisons Administration official told MEW that every prison has a bread oven, which makes bread for the prisoners and for sale to the outside.

[20]Undated letter, written in Arabic, received by Middle East Watch on November 1, 1992.

detained at Abu Za'bal in 1991 was indignant when describing his daily diet to MEW: "Foul with insects, lentils with stones! This was the food for the elite of Egypt—professors, sheiks, doctors, engineers and university students!"

From MEW's inspections, it appears that prisoners supplement their diet extensively with food supplied by their families, and that inmates pool these supplies and prepare collective meals. MEW observed families awaiting visits with boxes of carrots, tomatoes, oranges and bananas, as well as canned goods, sugar, tea and other goods. When interviewing families and prisoners during visits, MEW saw the exchange of boxes and took testimony from prisoners who indicated that the supplies were not usually intercepted by prison guards, except for routine inspections.

Prisoners from other countries—typically Africans—who receive no food from the outside, pointed out to MEW that they were dependent upon begging for donations from other inmates. The journey of a Nigerian national through the Egyptian prison system is illustrative:

> I stayed at the [el-Nooza] police station for three days. No food and nothing to sleep on was given to me....During the six months detention at Tora Prison, no food, sleeping materials, and medical care was given to me. The [Egyptians] also in detention get their daily food from their families. Myself being a foreigner had no family in Egypt and nobody to provide me with food. I had to beg for food from the Egyptian inmates....
>
> When I was sentenced and transferred to Abu Za'bal Prison for hard labor, the conditions became worse. *I was totally converted to a beggar by the prison system.* The prison provides only four slices of bread daily, seven grams of meat weekly, five grams of cheese and ninety-six grams of jam monthly, plus a bucket of white rice (about twenty-four liters) for a prison section of about nine hundred and sixty inmates....
>
> However, the prison made a provision where one can buy raw food, vegetables and other provisions to prepare

one's food. The Egyptian inmates are provided with job opportunities within the prison premises and are paid monthly from their families and friends who bring them enough food (both raw and cooked) that will last for the next fifteen days [until the next regular visit]. A foreigner is not provided with jobs in Abu Za'bal prison. Being far from home, one's parents and relatives find it difficult to visit one and provide one with one's basic needs. As a result of this, one turns to a beggar, begging for all one's needs from the indigenous inmates who give grudgingly and most of the times with insults and harshness....

Now...after completing my hard labor sentence in Abu Za'bal [and transferred to another prison], I have just discovered that the same system...applies here (no job, food, prison uniform, toilet articles, slippers, shoes, medicines and sleeping materials are provided).[21]

In addition to the difficult situation for imprisoned foreign nationals from poor families, another major consequence of the family-subsidized food-supply system is that inmates held in isolation—"in quarantine," say the authorities—at the beginning of their confinement or those held in punishment cells, also are reduced to a meager diet. The same problem is experienced by security detainees who are held for short periods and then released, because during the first month of detention no family visits are allowed and these detainees must rely solely on prison food. (See Chapter Three for additional information.) Obviously, the same situation prevails for other Egyptian prisoners whose families do not, or cannot, visit them on a regular basis.

It was difficult to determine if there are system-wide polices governing the number of times a day that prisoners were fed, and it

---

[21]Letter to MEW, dated April 1, 1992. Emphasis added.

appeared that this varied from prison to prison.[22] Prisoners in one cell in Abu Za'bal told MEW that they were fed twice a day, at 8:00 a.m. (foul and rice) and again at noon (lentils and rice). These prisoners were stewing a pot of lentils, supplemented by vegetables brought to them by visiting relatives, on a makeshift "stove" when MEW visited their cell. It was clear that, after the staple fare was distributed, these prisoners were free to cook meals at times of their choice. "We eat when we decide that we're hungry," one inmates said.

Inside the cells in almost every prison visited, MEW saw prisoners cooking food on tiny stoves, typically bricks with grooves cut out in which wire coils provided a heating element.[23] Some prisoners improvised even further, creating stoves with bare wire coils placed in sand-filled tin cans. Only in Tanta prison did MEW not find a prevalence of the makeshift stoves.[24] The obvious danger of the numerous exposed electric wires that power these stoves highlights the mixed blessing that they, and the makeshift wiring for electric lighting, produce. As one prisoner wrote to MEW:

> There are lots of naked electrical wires in the whole of the prisons. One Egyptian in room "4/6" [of Qanater Men's prison] died of electrical shock. Many inmates constantly get electrical shocks when they forget themselves and lean on naked wires.[25]

---

[22]At Tanta Prison, officials said that three meals are served to the prisoners daily: breakfast from at 7:00 or 8:00 a.m.; lunch at 12 noon; and dinner at 2:00 p.m. They said that all three meals include some combination of cheese, foul, lentils, rice, jam, meat, dates, and *tamiyya* (fried ground chick peas). MEW did not have the opportunity to independently confirm the regularity or content of this diet.

[23]One prisoner in Abu Za'bal's First Department indicated that these brick stoves could be purchased in Egyptian markets for LE 10, or about three dollars.

[24]While MEW could not ascertain any reason for the relatively fewer number of stoves at Tanta, it was pronounced.

[25]Letter to MEW, dated April 1, 1992.

One inmate in Qanater women's prison also noted that small fires have been caused by the makeshift wiring.

PUNISHING LIVING CONDITIONS FOR INCOMING SECURITY PRISONERS

MEW found that upon arrival at a prison, incoming security detainees often are held in cells—for weeks to over a month or more—in inferior conditions. These detainees also suffer from prolonged periods of daily lock-down (see Chapter Three) and denial of medical attention (see Chapter Five). This policy appears to be long-standing at Tora Istikbal, where many security detainees have been and continue to be held. For example, an engineer who was arrested in April 1989 was transferred on the third day to Tora Istikbal prison. Upon arrival, he told MEW that he was thoroughly and violently searched—"they even cut the seams of my clothes to be sure there was nothing inside." While he was being searched, he was also beaten. Then he was placed in a small solitary cell: "I was held there for two weeks. I never saw the sun. The cell door was never opened."[26] A political activist with the leftist Tagammu Party told of his arrest in August 1989. After being held six days at a Cairo police station, he was transferred to Abu Za'bal prison. He said that he and four other detainees were placed in a cell with no lights that was covered with spider webs. The prisoners gave cigarettes to the guards in exchange for several dirty blankets, and paid them money to obtain a light for the cell.[27]

Testimony taken from other former security detainees and corroborated during prison visits indicates that incoming security detainees assigned to the four-story Building A at Tora Istikbal are held in small 6x10 foot cells on the first floor. They typically are not allowed out of these cells for one month or more, before being moved to larger 10x15 foot cells on the second floor. The first-floor cells are deprived of light and ventilation due to the construction of a cinderblock wall that

---

[26]MEW interview, Mansoura, February 3, 1992.

[27]This detainee was released without charge after ten days at the prison. Interview by Dr. Robert S. Lawrence, Cairo, May 28, 1990.

runs parallel to the cells, creating a dark ten-foot-wide hallway that blocks the entry of light and air from the building's atrium. While not officially designated as punishment cells, these first-floor cells duplicate many of the conditions of punishment cells, in particular the long periods endured by detainees without time outside the cells. Moreover, inmates in these cells, unlike most prisoners held in punishment cells, must cope with severe overcrowding.

Because incoming security prisoners, like all other prisoners, do not receive family visits for the first thirty days after their arrival at a prison, they are denied benefits from the family-visit system which supplies Egyptian prisoners with needed bedding, supplemental food and specialized medicines. Conditions of detention therefore are especially punishing for short-term security detainees who are held for a month or so and then released without charge. As the testimony below indicates, in the first days and weeks after arrival of detainees at Abu Za'bal prison in October and November 1991, officials did not provide them with basic necessities such as mattresses, blankets or warm clothing. In some cases, its appears that the detainees were assigned to cells with particularly harsh physical conditions. Combined, these conditions constitute a form of unauthorized punishment.

● A Muslim cleric (*imam*) arrested in October 1991 was transferred to Abu Za'bal Industrial prison after several days in the custody of SSI. He spent three days in a cell on the ground floor that had no mattress or blankets. Then he was moved to a cell in a larger room upstairs, where it was very cold and no blankets were provided.

● Another teacher, who was also arrested in October 1991, was held incommunicado for five days in SSI custody and then moved to Abu Za'bal. He was put in a first-floor cell with no bedding or blankets, and then moved upstairs. "There was no mattress or blankets, the cell was full of insects, and there was no glass in the window," he told MEW.

● A second teacher, arrested in November 1991, experienced similar deprivations at Abu Za'bal after being transferred there from SSI custody.

> When we arrived, they took our money and identity cards. They made us bow down and a barber cut our hair. Then we were put in a dirty room on the first floor

with three permanently open windows. It was very cold
and there were no blankets—nothing.

His 6.5-by-13-foot cell held four inmates at first, then the number of
occupants increased to thirteen. He was held there for three days and
four nights, before being moved to a cell on the third floor.

● A Muslim Brotherhood leader in Alexandria was another one of those
rounded up at the time of the Madrid Middle East peace conference in
October 1991. He was held for two months at Abu Za'bal, where he said
that security detainees were treated "like animals." The water supply was
constantly interrupted, glass had been removed from the windows in the
third-floor cells, and there were cockroaches in the cells and in the
food.[28]

● In a separate interview, another Muslim Brotherhood activist from
Alexandria who was also arrested in October 1991 and held at Abu Za'bal,
provided additional information. After three days detention at a local
police station, where he slept on a tile floor with no mattress or blanket,
he was transferred to Abu Za'bal at night. He told MEW that detainees'
heads were completely shaved and, since only white garments were
allowed to be worn, their clothes were taken: "They handed out rags that
had been worn by others." He said that prison personnel used extremely
insulting and obscene language with the detainees: "Human beings simply
have no value there," he said with disgust."I was put in a cell on the
ground floor that had no windows, no blankets. The next day I was
moved upstairs." There, he shared a 20-by-30-foot cell with thirty-five
other men, all Muslim Brothers: "It was very dark in the cell. There
were no windows, and there was glass all over the floor. Water dripped
from the ceiling, and the room was full of cockroaches and lots of
insects."

He said that the door to the cell was kept closed all the time. On
occasion, prison officers would barge into the cell and force the detainees
to sit in squatting positions on the floor. "Once they forced us to squat
for one hour," he said, noting that the older men had found this "very
tiring." The detainees also were periodically subjected to what was called

---

[28]MEW interview, Alexandria, February 1, 1992.

"the search." They were not permitted to have newspapers, pens or paper, and were told that they would be punished if newspapers were discovered. "They would search the cell, and tear up any paper and break any pens they found."[29]

---

[29]*Ibid.*

3
DAILY LOCK-DOWN

"We were not allowed outside our cell except for five minutes in the morning, when we could walk in the corridor. They called this the picnic."

> — Muslim Brotherhood activist from Alexandria, describing his confinement at Abu Za'bal prison to MEW in February 1992.

"There is no air in this cell. We never see the sun. We asked so many times for one hour or even a half-hour outside every day, but no way. We get no exercise—all our muscles are atrophied."

> — Woman prisoner completing a three-year sentence at Qanater, Egypt's largest women's prison, interviewed by MEW in February 1992.

During MEW's visits to prisons, officials stressed that inmates were allowed out of their cells for at least one hour daily. For most male prisoners in facilities MEW visited, this policy appeared to be in effect. In fact, many inmates reported that the daily time outside their cells extended, typically, from about 8:00 in the morning until various times in the mid-afternoon.

Particularly for prisoners who are confined in extremely overcrowded cells, the time allowed outside each day is a welcome—and necessary—relief. But for many prisoners, security and criminal alike, time *outside* their cells did not mean time *outdoors* in fresh air and sunlight. Cells simply were unlocked and inmates permitted to walk around in interior atriums. Women prisoners, in contrast, complained that they were rarely let out of their extremely crowded dormitory cells at all (see Chapter Eight). These conditions are in flagrant violation of minimum international standards, which require at least one hour of exercise in the open air daily for all prisoners not engaged in outdoor work.[1]

From prison to prison, and even within the same facility, MEW found considerable variations in the amount of time prisoners were allowed out of their cells on a daily basis. The most serious complaint about confinement came from security prisoners, who spent long hours locked inside their cells. Some security prisoners held without charge at Tora Istikbal told MEW that they had not been let out of their small cells for months at a time.

DISPARITY IN TREATMENT OF
LONG-TERM SECURITY DETAINEES

At two prisons, Tora Istikbal and Abu Za'bal Liman, MEW found wide disparities between security and criminal prisoners—and among various groups of security prisoners—in the time allotted for them to be outside their cells. At Tora Istikbal, almost 500 unsentenced long-term security detainees suffered the most from extensive daily confinement inside overcrowded cells.

Tora Istikbal

Unsentenced security prisoners and sentenced criminal prisoners at Tora Istikbal are held in separate sections of two four-story atrium-style buildings of modern construction. MEW was not allowed to see Building B and only visited Building A, which held 264 security prisoners "under investigation," housed on the first two floors (with the exception of five men whom the authorities said had requested to be placed upstairs) and 306 criminal prisoners occupying cells on the third and fourth floors.

Prison officials indicated that the criminal prisoners were allowed outside their cells from 8:00 a.m. to 2:30 p.m. each day. Interviews showed that the time out of the cells afforded to security prisoners in Building A varied from none to forty-five minutes a day. Repeated

---

[1]United Nations Minimum Rules, Article 21(1).

testimonies indicated that inmates are generally deprived of time outside their cells for the first thirty days of their imprisonment. As one inmate put it, "You are alone with nothing. There are no family visits for the first thirty days." For some inmates, solitary confinement continues longer. The occupant of Cell Forty-Nine on the first floor of Tora Istikbal, where prisoners live in sixty cells with solid steel doors that have no opening or peephole, shouted to MEW representatives as they walked along the corridor that he had not been outside his cell for sixty days. Four men in another cell said that they had been held there since October 1991—about four months—and "not once" had been outside their cell.

Security detainees on the second floor were allowed forty-five minutes a day out of their cells. The area in which the detainees were allowed to walk was no more than 8-by-100 feet and devoid of sunlight. With the men from eight overcrowded cells sharing this small space at any one time (due to staggering), the daily forty-five-minute break afforded very little opportunity for exercise. A detainee interviewed on the second floor told MEW that some detainees on the first floor were not allowed out of their cells for over sixty days, adding that in all cases no one was allowed out of these cells for the first thirty days. On the second floor, MEW found eleven men in a cell that measured about 10x10 feet. One had been there for twenty months and another for nineteen months. "Some people have been on this floor for over two years," one of the detainees said. MEW inspected another cell of the same size with ten occupants. One of them, a twenty-six-year-old from Alexandria, had been held there for seventeen months, and another, a twenty-five-year-old from Cairo, for thirteen months.

According to testimonies, in Building B some detainees are continuously locked in the first-floor cells for two to three months. EOHR has called continuous closed confinement "the most prevalent abuse in the Tora Complex." It reported in 1991 that newly arrived detainees were kept locked inside their cells for the first month. EOHR charged that "this is done ...merely as a means to undermine their morale and break their spirit."[2]

---

[2]EOHR, "Human Rights Violations in Egyptian Prisons: The Model of the Tora Prisons Complex," August 1991, p. 7.

This prolonged daily confinement was a major issue in the hunger strike that was in progress by the security detainees when MEW visited Tora Istikbal.[3] We received many handwritten petitions from the strikers, all of them demanding a change in the confinement policy. "We request a break from 8:00 in the morning until 4:00 in the afternoon," several notes read. Other petitions demanded the "sun parade" (*thabur as-shams*) in the prison yard. "The break is very short, and we don't see the sun," one detainee wrote.

Abu Za'bal Liman

In Abu Za'bal Liman, the maximum-security prison, sentenced criminal prisoners were allowed out of their cells for several hours in the morning and afternoon. One prisoner serving a twenty-year narcotics sentence told MEW that his group cell was opened from 8:00 a.m. to 4:00 p.m. daily. Another prisoner, in a separate interview, said that his 120-men cell in the Third Department was opened daily from 8:30 to 3:00 p.m.

Yet in the First Department of Abu Za'bal, Palestinian security detainees—who have not been charged or sentenced for any offense, and some of whom have been held for over two years—reported to MEW that they were allowed out of their terribly overcrowded cells and into the indoor atrium courtyard area for only ninety minutes in the morning and ninety minutes in the afternoon. In contrast, other prisoners in the First Department told MEW that they were permitted in the courtyard area from approximately 8:00 in the morning until 3:00 in the afternoon.

---

[3]MEW visited Tora Istikbal on February 16, 1992. Prison officials told MEW that the hunger strike had started on February 13, but some detainees told MEW that they had stopped eating on February 9, while others said they had stopped eating on February 11. In no case did any striking detainee agree with the authorities' contention that the strike was only in its fourth day at the time of MEW's visit.

LENGTHY LOCK-DOWN OF SENTENCED SECURITY PRISONERS

MEW also took complaints about lengthy periods of cell confinement from sentenced security prisoners at Tora Liman. One prisoner, sentenced in 1989, told MEW:

> I arrived at Tora Liman and was put in a solitary cell for eight months. Every two days, I was allowed out of the cell for ten minutes. Then it was increased to fifteen minutes for four months. Then twenty minutes for two or three months. In the last few months, the treatment has been less severe. I think that the government is trying to do better, because of the pressure.

In a separate interview, another prisoner in the same compound agreed:

> After Amnesty International's last report,[4] about two or three months ago, things started to improve. We are now let out in the courtyard from 8:00 a.m. to 2:00 p.m. I think this is only temporary. I don't believe it will last.

Prisoners serving sentences for membership in the banned Jihad Organization, housed in another section of Tora Liman, also have been subjected to lengthy periods of confinement and other punitive practices. Although at the time of MEW's visit, the prisoners said they were let out of their cells from 8:00 a.m. to 2:30 p.m. daily, one of them remarked: "If something happens on the outside, we are punished. When a police officer was killed in Ain Shams a few years ago, we were confined to our cells for three months." (These prisoners had previously been confined to their cells for several years, a practice which led to a court case and a ruling in January 1992; see Chapter Four.)

Tora Liman prison houses suspects held under investigation in connection with the 1990 assassination of Rifat el-Mahgoub, the speaker of Egypt's Parliament. One of these suspects told MEW that he was transferred to the liman in May 1991 from Tora Istikbal. For the first

---

[4]The prisoner is referring to "Egypt: Ten Years of Torture," published by Amnesty International in October 1991.

five months, he was allowed outside his cell, which had no plumbing facilities, for only ten minutes each morning to collect water and empty the bucket that served as a toilet. "I was really being punished with solitary confinement," he said. Then, beginning in January 1992, these prisoners were allowed out of their cells for two hours a day, in groups of five.

Short-Term Security Prisoners

MEW interviewed numerous former security prisoners who had been detained for one to three months, without charge, in the aftermath of the round-ups of security suspects at the time of the Middle East peace conference in Madrid in October 1991. Some of these former detainees—many of them engineers, teachers, accountants and other professionals affiliated with the Muslim Brotherhood—complained about the limited time they were permitted outside their cells.

One activist from Alexandria, arrested in October 1991, was held in Abu Za'bal prison in a second-floor cell measuring about 20-by-30 feet shared by thirty-five other men, all of them Muslim Brothers. He told MEW: "We were not allowed outside our cell except for five minutes in the morning, when we could walk in the corridor. They called this the picnic."[5] Former member of parliament Hassan el-Gamal, who served from 1979 to 1989, was arrested in October 1991 and spent fifteen days at Tora Istikbal. He was held for the first week in a small cell on the ground floor with two other men. There was no water source in the cell except from a pipe on the ceiling with a hole in it. The hole was plugged with a piece of wood, and the men removed the wood to get water. "For the first week, we were not allowed out of this cell once," el-Gamal told MEW. The type of confinement for short-term security prisoners in their cells at Tora Istikbal appears to be a long-standing practice. An engineer who was held on the first floor in April 1989 told MEW: "I was placed in an 8x10 foot cell where, for two weeks, I did not see the sun and was not let out at all."[6]

---

[5]MEW interview, Alexandria, February 1, 1992.

[6]MEW interview, Mansoura, February 3, 1992.

TIME OUTSIDE CELLS FOR NON-SECURITY PRISONERS

For most prisoners MEW interviewed, the daily time they are allowed outside their cells does not include time outdoors in the open air, as required by international standards. In no case did MEW find that the prisoners held in these sections were allowed to go outdoors into the prison yard or otherwise to leave the building, except for family visits.

Tanta Prison

Male inmates in Tanta live in two four-story, rectangular-shaped brick buildings. The buildings are identical in design and are located parallel to one another, separated by a large and barren dirt courtyard. The buildings have an atrium design, with an open roof over a long interior courtyard with a tile floor. The cells on each floor are configured along both sides of the length of the interior courtyard.

The commander of Tanta prison told MEW that inmates were let out of their cells all day, except from 12:00 noon to 2:00 p.m. when they were counted and fed. He added that in the winter they were let out at about 7:00 a.m. and returned at about 5:00 p.m. In the summer, the time outside reportedly was extended to 7 p.m. The prison director claimed that the approximately 50-by-200-foot open area between the two buildings was used as a sports field and activity area. However, he contradicted himself as we walked onto the field and noticed pools of sewage and stagnant water, saying that prisoners do not get to go into the yard: "Only workers go into the yard because of security reasons; the prisoners go out of their rooms but remain inside the buildings." He revised this assertion seconds later when one of his officers mentioned that time outside might be a subject of MEW's report, saying: "They have an hour outside."

But there were no visible signs in the yard that 2,000 men or even 250 men regularly occupied the open area. There were no foot prints in the dust or even in the mud that would indicate anyone had walked there recently. There was a crust on the top of the ground apparently formed by rapidly drying mud due to receding water that had not been broken by footprints. There were no sports equipment or facilities, or any other indication of any activity conducted outside.

Once inside Tanta's dormitory buildings, prisoners told MEW that the commander was mistaken and that they never were allowed outdoors. Six men held in one cell, all under investigation for forgery, said that they generally were let out of their cells from 8:00 to 11:30 a.m. and 1:00 to 4:00 p.m. to walk around in the interior atrium, but that inmates "never" went outdoors.

Abu Za'bal Liman

The First Department of Abu Za'bal Liman is a three-story, atrium-type building that was constructed in the early 1970's, with the cells of the second and third floors open onto the atrium courtyard in the center of the building. All of the cells on the right side of the first floor, and half of those on the left, are cut off from the courtyard's light and air by a brick wall which forms a hallway in front of the cell doors. In the First Department, prisoner mobility outside their cells is limited to certain sections of the balcony-like walkways that overlook the interior courtyard. Prisoners—with the notable exception of the Palestinian detainees discussed above—told MEW that they were let out of their cells from 7:00 in the morning to 3:00 in the afternoon.

The Third and Fourth Departments of Abu Za'bal Liman are in separate, walled-off sections, each with five one-story buildings. Inmates in these departments told MEW that they were let out of their cells on a daily basis and allowed into department courtyard areas daily from approximately 8:00 in the morning until 2:00 or 3:00 in the afternoon. There, they could walk around, take in the sun, or make use of an outdoor water basin.

Tora Mazraa

Tora Mazraa consists of four sections, each with two one-story buildings with dormitory cells opening onto a single walkway. MEW observed the liberal access that prisoners had to various parts of this facility. Prisoners were able to leave their own cells, go into the main prison courtyard, and enter the buildings and dormitory cells in other sections.

4
AUTHORIZED DISCIPLINARY MEASURES AND UNAUTHORIZED PUNISHMENT

"I was beaten once. I was taken out into the big hall and about forty soldiers encircled me. I turned and they hit me with electric sticks. The sticks were about forty to fifty centimeters long, black with plastic. It lasted for about ten minutes. They hit me on the head and I collapsed. This group is called 'the beating force.'"

> *— University student describing an incident at Tora Istikbal prison during his detention there from October to December 1991.*

Egyptian law permits the beating of juvenile prisoners and the whipping of adult prisoners as a disciplinary penalty. Both practices are proscribed by the Egyptian Constitution and are clear violations of international law. International rules for the treatment of prisoners prohibit corporal punishment for disciplinary offenses.[1] In addition to this authorized physical abuse, MEW found compelling evidence that male inmates in Egyptian prisons have been beaten and whipped in a variety of situations other than in meting out authorized punishment. Most alarming about the physical violence we documented is that some of it clearly was premeditated and organized, carried out in the presence of prison officers.

MEW also found that security detainees held without charge for both short and long terms, and sentenced security prisoners, are singled out for forms of treatment that constitute unauthorized punishment.

---

[1] Article 31 of the Minimum Rules states: "Corporal punishment, punishment by placing in a dark cell, and all cruel, inhuman or degrading punishments shall be completely prohibited as punishments for disciplinary offences." Similarly, such punishments are prohibited by the International Covenant on Civil and Political Rights and the Convention Against Torture and Other Cruel, Inhuman or Degrading Treatment or Punishment. Egypt is a state party to both treaties.

Under Egyptian law, prisoners can be placed in solitary confinement for up to fifteen days for each disciplinary offense. In inspections of the punishment wings of prisons and during interviews with randomly selected inmates held in punishment cells, MEW discovered appalling physical conditions, wide discrepancies in the amount of time that prisoners were permitted outside punishment cells on a daily basis, and other kinds of poor treatment. MEW also found examples of the use of punishment cells for unauthorized purposes, including one instance in which a teenage prisoner was confined to a small barren cell "for psychological treatment" and another in which a young detainee was placed in a punishment cell because he refused to confess to a criminal offense.

Egyptian human rights monitors have been very critical of solitary confinement in prisons. In a 1991 report, EOHR argued that solitary confinement in punishment cells is imposed without procedural safeguards on its use and without regard for the effects of the punishment.[2] EOHR recommended that the punishment of solitary confinement be abolished or its use severely limited. Short of abolition of the practice, EOHR argued that solitary confinement should be limited "so that it will not exceed three days, and then only on the basis of a judicial order issued ... after an investigation by the public prosecution" during which the prisoner would be allowed to present a defense. EOHR would also require written certification from a doctor that the prisoner can withstand the punishment.[3]

---

[2]"The penalty of solitary confinement is imposed on the prisoner without questioning him or submitting him to a medical examination, as is stipulated by prison statutes, nor is the prisoner submitted to the daily medical examination further stipulated in the statutes to determine the possible detrimental effects of the punishment." EOHR, "Prisons in Egypt: The Model of the Tora Prisons Complex," p. 8.

[3]Ibid., p. 16.

INFORMING PRISONERS OF DISCIPLINARY RULES

Under Article 19 of the 1956 law governing prisons, disciplinary offenses include: disobeying the orders of the prison commander or other officers; lack of respect for employees and visitors at the prison; refusal to work or laziness regarding work; cursing or issuing threats; immoral actions and gestures; violating the rights of others or attacking others; disturbing the peace of the prison by creating noise; leaving designated areas without reason; inflicting physical damage on prison facilities; urinating or defecating anywhere except places designated for these purposes; and possessing prohibited materials.[4]

International standards specify that literate inmates should be given written notice about the prison's regulations and discipline.[5] MEW found that in Egypt, prisoners are not supplied with written rules when they arrive at an institution, although officials insisted that prisoners are adequately informed orally of the grounds upon which they may be subject to punishment.

The director of Abu Za'bal Liman, Gen. Mustafa Thabet, told MEW that new prisoners are informed about the prison's rules orally, upon arrival at the prison.[6]   Gen. Lutfi, the highest-ranking

---

[4] Cited in Khalil and Salem, *Prisons in Egypt*.

[5] Article 35(1) of the Minimum Rules states: "Every prisoner on admission shall be provided written information about the regulations governing the treatment of prisoners of his category, the disciplinary requirements of the institution, the authorized methods of seeking information and making complaints and all such other matters as are necessary to enable him to understand both his rights and his obligations and to adapt himself to the life of the institution."

[6] Gen. Thabet said: "The prisoner is told what he needs to do to avoid discipline. They are taken to my office, where I personally go through the prisoner's papers and decide in which of the several Abu Za'bal prisons they will be placed. The officer of the prison to which the prisoner is assigned then takes custody of the prisoner, and explains the rules to the prisoner." MEW interview, February 12, 1992.

investigations officer in the Prisons Administration, also told MEW that the rules are laid out to incoming prisoners orally, not in writing. When a prisoner first arrives, "officers have a discussion with him, telling him what is permitted and what is not." Gen. Lutfi added that the prisons have written rules and procedures, and that any officer or guard receives a brief training session on how to work in prison.[7] But the lack of written rules creates confusion—and frustration—for prisoners, such as the inmate at Qanater men's prison who wrote to Middle East Watch: "We have reached a stage where we no longer know what is permitted or prohibited in this jail. One official will permit something and when another one comes, he will prohibit it. We do not know which one to follow."[8]

AUTHORIZED PUNISHMENT:
CONFINEMENT IN PUNISHMENT CELLS

Solitary confinement for the purpose of punishment is legally authorized in Egyptian prisons, with up to fifteen days confinement permitted for each disciplinary offense.[9] All of the prisons that MEW visited had separate punishment wings. The wings were similar in design from prison to prison, usually consisting of a row or several rows of adjacent, small single cells in an area walled off from other parts of the prison. Because prisoners punished by solitary confinement typically are denied family visits, they are deprived of supplemental food and must rely solely on prison rations. Most of them also appear to be deprived of any personal effects from their regular cells. Former and current inmates of punishment cells complained to MEW about poor food, inadequate bedding and clothing (especially when the weather was cold), and deplorable sanitary conditions.

---

[7]MEW interview, February 13, 1992.

[8]Letter dated October 28, 1992.

[9]Article 44(4) of Law 396 of 1956, cited in EOHR, "Prisons in Egypt: The Model of the Tora Prisons Complex," p. 4.

Living Conditions

The living conditions in occupied punishment cells inspected by MEW were especially harsh. Not one punishment cell inspected by MEW had a toilet or running water—inmates were forced to use buckets for toilets and plastic bottles of water for drinking. One of the cells visited contained only two filthy prison-issue grey blankets and one small metal bucket, which served as the inmate's toilet. The cell had no plumbing and no sink. The odor emanating from the dark cell was overpowering when the door was opened by prison officials. There were piles of feces along the rear wall of the 6x10-foot room, which did not have a light bulb.

The interiors of most punishment cells inspected by MEW were bare, with cement or stone walls and floors. A small window positioned high on the wall above the door provided little ventilation and natural light.

MEW inspected three of the punishment cells at Tora Liman prison, called the "new cells" by inmates. Each cell measures about 5-by-10 feet, with fifteen-foot-high ceilings and a 3-by-4-foot skylight. The doors are constructed of heavy wood, with a small 4-by-6-inch opening. There is a single, small, 1-by-2-foot window located ten feet above the floor of each cell, providing almost no light. The bare cement floors of the cells were covered with dirt. There was nothing else in the cells except a bucket and a blanket. Cell Fifteen was empty except for the single blanket on which its lone inmate slept. There was one light bulb in the cell, hanging from frayed wires.

Cell Thirteen, which housed three inmates, had only one blanket. There was a water bottle and a little food— several pieces of Egyptian flat bread and about two cups of cooked rice. The room was completely dark: the small window allowed in no light and the skylight in the ceiling was covered. The cement floor was covered with a quarter-inch layer of dirt and ten or so cigarette butts. (MEW found punishment cells that were occupied by more than one prisoner only at Tora Liman. All of the cells in the punishment wing were occupied, and four were grossly overcrowded. Cells Ten, Eleven, Thirteen, and Nineteen housed three inmates each, while all the other cells inspected by MEW held only one inmate each. Prison officials told MEW that two prisoners were never placed in a single cell in order "to discourage homosexual activity.")

The bathroom serving the punishment wing, a 15-by-8-foot room in the center of the punishment area, had five toilet stalls. Two of the toilet stalls were completely flooded with sewage when MEW inspected them and the whole room reeked of urine and feces. The air in this nearly completely dark room was damp and cold. A water pipe running along the wall leaked, covering the floor with a half-inch layer of muddy water. The severely cracked and broken cement floor was slippery, covered with mud and algae. In both corners of the room were uncovered buckets of spoiled garbage. Nearby, the washroom's cement trough basin was filled with stagnant water.

The one-story men's punishment wing at Tanta General Prison contains twelve cells. The authorities said that eight of the cells were occupied at the time of MEW's visit. Each cell, measuring about 6.5-by-10 feet, has a concrete floor. All the peepholes on the doors of the cells were covered, with the exception of the door to one cell that was unoccupied and used for storage. A prison official explained the covering-up of the peepholes by saying it was done "so prohibited substances cannot be put through the openings."

Time Outside Cells

MEW found that some prisoners are not allowed outside punishment cells for days at a time, while others receive a daily "break" ranging from five to thirty minutes. Because punishment cells lack running water and toilet facilities, time outside the cells is critically important so that prisoners can attend to personal hygiene needs. At one prison, officials said that prisoners were allowed out of the punishment cells for two hours daily, but occupants of the cells interviewed by MEW said that the daily time outside was no more than five minutes.

Tora Liman

Prison officials at Tora Liman insisted that inmates in punishment cells are released for thirty minutes per day to use the washroom's toilet and shower. MEW interviewed several current occupants of punishment cells who confirmed this practice.[10] But other prisoners interviewed by MEW said that the policy was not uniformly applied. One prisoner pointed out to MEW that the cards on the cell doors were of different colors. He said that prisoners with white cards were allowed out of their cells for at least thirty minutes a day, often longer, while prisoners with reddish-colored cards were not allowed outside their cells at all, except every several days to empty the buckets they used as toilets. Of the thirty-two prisoners held on the day of MEW's visit, twelve had reddish-colored cards in their doors.

In random interviews of occupants of punishment cells in the liman, MEW did not meet any prisoner who claimed he was never let out of his cell. But, in separate interviews, several prisoners complained that they had been locked in their cells for several days without being let out to use the washroom. One complained that the door to his cell was opened only every three to four days, to allow him to empty the bucket he used for a toilet. He said that he had been deprived of all food for three to four days and received water, which he collected in an empty one-liter soda bottle, only as often. He said that both food and water, when provided, were simply poured through the 4-by-6-inch hole in his door without regard for how he might be able to catch it. This practice apparently is not new at Tora Liman. In a separate interview, a prisoner at Tora Liman who had been held for four months in a punishment cell, beginning in August 1989, told MEW: "Food and water were poured through the one small peephole and onto the floor. I had to do my best to catch it."

Abu Za'bal Liman

Inmates in the punishment wing at Abu Za'bal Liman said that they were allowed out of their cells every day, for thirty minutes in the morning.

---

[10]One said that he was allowed out of his cell for thirty minutes a day "to fill my bottles of water." Another said he was permitted to leave his cell for twenty to thirty minutes daily.

Tanta General Prison

Officials told MEW that prisoners in the punishment wing are let out of their cells twice a day, for one hour in the morning and one hour in the afternoon, "one by one, for security reasons." Prisoners in the punishment wing told MEW a different story. The occupant of one cell had been held there for six days. "They let us come out to get our food and to go to the toilet," he said. He had not been out of his cell for more than five minutes every morning and five minutes each afternoon. Another prisoner had been there for eight days. The small room contained only two grey blankets. This prisoner, too, had not been outside the cell since his arrival. "I had a fight, someone took my cigarettes," he said, explaining why he was being punished. He said that he had been allowed to leave the cell only for "minutes, just to get my food in the morning and the afternoon. I cannot use the toilet or wash myself. There is no time."

Other Forms of Abuse in Punishment Cells

In random inspections of punishment wings, MEW found five cases that violated the Egyptian prison system's own rules, two of them involving women inmates. MEW discovered a teenage sentenced prisoner held for "treatment" of mental illness; a teenage detainee who refused to confess to the criminal offense for which he was arrested; and a prisoner held weeks beyond the legal limit of fifteen days confinement. At Qanater women's prison, one occupant of a punishment cell claimed that she had been held there for five months, serving a six-month punishment term. Also in Qanater's punishment wing was a fifty-year-old housewife, a security detainee, who told MEW she had been locked in her cell for seventeen days (see Chapter Eight).[11]

---

[11]Prison officials told MEW that security detainees are sometimes placed in solitary cells in the punishment wings of prisons to keep them separated from other prisoners. At Tanta Prison, MEW interviewed a veterinarian, arrested and detained without charge under the Emergency Law, who had been transferred to Tanta general prison after ten days of incommunicado detention at an SSI office. Upon arrival at the prison, he was placed in a cell in the punishment wing. He was allowed significantly greater liberties than the inmates who were in the cells expressly for punishment. He told MEW that he was allowed out of his cell from 8:00 a.m. to 12 noon and from 1:00 to 4:00 p.m. daily, just like

For "Psychological Treatment"

During MEW's inspection of the punishment wing at Abu Za'bal Liman, MEW representatives heard singing coming from Cell Fourteen. When a MEW representative asked the prison director to open this cell for inspection, he said that the inmate was "crazy" and had been placed in the punishment cell the day before on orders of the prison doctor because he could not get along with his cellmates. The director emphasized that the eighteen-year-old inmate was "seen every Monday in the hospital clinic by a doctor specialized in mental problems." The prisoner's file indicated that he had been sentenced to six months imprisonment for theft on November 26, 1991 and was transferred from al-Marg prison to the liman "for psychological treatment." The file noted that he was placed in the punishment cell on February 11. MEW visited on February 12.

The cell, its skylight blocked off, was devoid of furnishings except for one thin blankets and a tin can that served as a toilet. The prisoner, who came out blinking from the light after the darkness of his cell, appeared disoriented, and also surprised at the group of strangers and prison officials at his door. He incoherently answered several questions put to him by a MEW representative, and then mumbled: "I'm hungry now." Prison officials told MEW that he was about to be fed dinner. The prisoner had a plastic bottle of water that was almost empty.

The assignment of this prisoner to a punishment cell was obviously a grave breach of minimum international standards, which specify that prisoners "who suffer from...mental diseases or abnormalities shall be observed and treated in specialized institutions under medical supervision."[12]

---

prisoners in the main buildings, and was allowed to have personal belongings in his cell. However, the conditions of confinement imposed on the woman security detainee whom MEW found in the punishment wing at Qanater were in marked contrast to those experienced by the veterinarian.

[12]Article 82(2) of the United Nations Minimum Rules.

For Refusing to Confess

MEW found one young detainee at Tanta prison who had been placed in a punishment cell after he refused to confess to a criminal offense. He occupied one of the twelve cells in the punishment wing that MEW had randomly selected for inspection. In a private interview, out of earshot of prison officials, he said that he had been arrested the previous month, accused of a criminal offense. He said that a prison officer used force to attempt to coerce a confession almost immediately after his arrival at the prison:

> An officer came and took me from my cell [in Building A] to his office. He tried to make me confess to stealing and doing other things. I refused to confess. He told me that he would give me time to think and would call for me the next day. On the second day, I told him that I had nothing for him. So he brought me here [to the punishment cell] and hit me for ten minutes.

This detainee's cell had only two blankets, and a bucket for a toilet. He said that he was fed twice a day—bread and foul in the morning, and rice and lentils in the afternoon. He had one plastic bottle that was filled with water. The card on the door of his cell said he was being disciplined with three days of isolation punishment, beginning on February 14, for "not participating in prison activities." MEW met this detainee on February 19. There was no notation on his card explaining why he had been held beyond the three days of punishment. "They just gave me three more days," the teenager said.

Confinement Beyond the Authorized Punishment Period

MEW found three prisoners who had been held in punishment cells beyond the maximum fifteen days authorized by law. At Tora Liman, MEW interviewed one occupant of a punishment cell who pointed to the small index-sized cards attached to the outside doors of the punishment cells and said that the cards indicated the length of time a prisoner was sentenced to the punishment area. He complained that he was scheduled to be released on January 3, 1992, after serving the maximum fifteen days permitted under the law, but—some forty days later—he still had not been returned to his regular cell. When MEW queried prison officials about this, they tried to explain by saying that the original date on the card was not the day of release but the day on which the prisoner's status was re-evaluated.

Regarding this prisoner's complaint, Gen. Mustafa Lufti, the top inspection official in the Prisons Administration, admitted that he did not know why the prisoner was still being held in the punishment cell, but assured MEW that he would check the prisoner's file. (According to Gen. Lufti, the prisoner's card indicated that he had been committed to the punishment cell for possession of drugs in prison.)

The other two prisoners held in punishment cells longer than the authorized fifteen-day maximum were at Qanater women's prison (see Chapter Eight).

Other Complaints
In addition to complaints about extremely limited periods of daily time outside the punishment cells, some prisoners noted other instances of poor treatment by the authorities. In separate interviews, occupants of some punishment cells at Tora Liman told MEW that they had been denied food and water for several days at a time, and had been subjected to mistreatment by guards.

A sentenced criminal prisoner in his early twenties told MEW that he had recently been transferred to Tora Liman after serving over two years in another liman. He told MEW that it was "impossible to believe the extent to which we are treated badly here." He said that upon his arrival at Tora Liman one month earlier, he had been placed in the punishment cell and had been confined there ever since. He complained that during the first few days he was beaten, and urinated and defecated upon by guards; after that, the beatings continued. He predicted that when MEW concluded its visit, he would be beaten again for speaking to MEW representatives.

Sentenced security prisoners at Tora Liman told MEW of incidents in which prison guards subjected inmates to inhumane and degrading conditions in punishment cells. In separate interviews, several Jihad prisoners complained of conditions in punishment cells to which they were taken "for any mistake." They described the cells as "dirty rooms without anything," where prisoners were deprived of food and water and generally held for two weeks. One described what he called a "particularly insidious" instance of abuse in the punishment cells:

> In 1988, Ibrahim Abdel Aziz, a lieutenant responsible for discipline here at the prison—who now is at Tora Istikbal—developed a new way of getting us to renounce our political ideas. He would send us to the punishment cell and they would then fill the floor of the cell with excrement and urine and have us stay there.

Other prisoners were placed in cells with water on the floor for several days. They were unable to sleep under these conditions, and become very cold from standing in the water for extended periods.

ARBITRARY USE OF PUNISHMENT MEASURES AGAINST SECURITY PRISONERS

There is substantial evidence that prison officials impose particularly harsh living conditions on sentenced security prisoners and security detainees held without charge under the Emergency Law for either short or long terms. MEW believes that these conditions rise to the level of deliberate collective punishment. Particularly harsh disciplinary measures are often applied to security prisoners without their having committed any disciplinary infractions. MEW documented various practices, ranging from the long-term sequestering of Islamist security detainees in an improvised punishment wing at Tora Istikbal prison, to especially punishing living conditions for incoming security prisoners at Tora Istikbal and Abu Za'bal prisons (described in Chapters Two and Three). In January 1992, an Egyptian court ruled that the authorities at Tora Liman prison violated the law by subjecting sentenced "Jihad" prisoners to prolonged solitary confinement and denial of newspapers, books and other items.

The Improvised Punishment Wing at Tora Istikbal

MEW discovered that a group of long-term Islamist security detainees have been continuously confined in an improvised punishment area of Tora Istikbal prison that inmates call "The Hospital." MEW representatives' requests to inspect "The Hospital" during their visit to

Tora Istikbal were repeatedly denied by the prison commander and other officials. According to former prisoners interviewed by MEW, this improvised punishment wing is located in Tora Istikbal's two-story administration building, on the second floor above the director's office. It acquired its name because the area was originally designed to house the prison's hospital.

When MEW representatives were leaving Tora Istikbal's Building A, they noticed three prisoners on stretchers in a large empty room off a wide corridor. The three men were participants in the hunger strike in progress by Islamist detainees, mentioned earlier. They were in the room to receive medical assistance. One of them, Mahmoud Muhammed Ahmad Shayeb, was a resident of "The Hospital" and, despite his obvious weakness, consented to speak with MEW in the presence of prison officials. He provided information about conditions in this improvised punishment area:

> Fourteen of us are being held in "The Hospital." Hassan Gharabawi has been there for three years, entering his fourth year. Some of us have been there for one to one and a half years. It is one room, about sixteen square meters (about 177 square feet). We never see the sun. Most of us have scabies.

None of the long-term detainees in "The Hospital" have been charged with an offense. Despite successive court-ordered releases, they have been held continuously by means of successive administrative detention orders issued by the Minister of Interior. In addition, they were held in "The Hospital" even though they had not committed disciplinary infractions while in prison. Tora Istikbal's director, Gen. Muhammad Awad, and Gen. Lufti of the Prisons Administration candidly admitted to MEW that the men held in "The Hospital" are "the leaders" and that they were confined there to prevent mingling with other prisoners whom they might influence.

Prolonged Solitary Confinement of "Jihad" Prisoners at Tora Liman

In September 1989, four sentenced "Jihad" prisoners at Tora Liman brought a lawsuit against Egyptian government officials and two prison commanders, challenging their prolonged solitary confinement and other practices, such as prohibiting the prisoners from having newspapers, magazines, books and radios.[13]

Several of these prisoners told MEW that, throughout their continuous confinement, they were subjected to additional punishing conditions. The electricity in the cells was turned off, depriving them of electric light and making the cells dark due to the small size and high position of the windows. All reading material was confiscated, and prisoners studying for degrees had their course work postponed. Family visits were denied and personal clothing and other items were confiscated. Prisoners were forced to rely only on the sparse supplies distributed by the prison. They had no supplemental food, clothing or bedding. In the winter there was no heat, which at the time of MEW's visit was provided by makeshift cooking elements.

The Administrative Judicial Court of Egypt's State Council ruled in the case on January 14, 1992, finding that the practices of the prison authorities violated Egyptian law.[14] In a memorandum to the court, the prison commander did not dispute that the prisoners had been held for several years in solitary confinement, but stated that this was because they were "dangerous, because of a prior escape by three of them on July 17, 1988, the precedents of threatening and attacking the guards and workers in the prison, and inciting disturbances in the liman." The commander further stated that the periods of solitary confinement "were renewed because of the lack of responsiveness of the prisoners to the rehabilitation programs and *the occurrence of incidents of attack by some of them on the guards and workers in the prison.*"[15] He noted that the

---

[13]The plaintiffs—Aboud Abd al-Latif Zumour, Fouad Mahmoud Hanafi, Tareq Abd al-Mojoud al-Zumour and Assam Abd al-Magid Muhammed Nagi—brought the case against the Minister of Interior, the director of the Prisons Administration, the director of the Tora prisons complex, and the commander of Tora Liman prison.

[14]Verdict concerning Case No. 7520/43Q, State Council (*maglis al-dawla*), Administrative Judicial Court, Individual Disputes Department "A." MEW translation of the original Arabic.

[15]Emphasis added.

prisoners were allowed out of their solitary cells for thirty minutes daily "under sufficient security."

The court rejected the prison authorities' reasons for placing the prisoners in prolonged solitary confinement. It ruled that the law "permits placing prisoners in solitary confinement only as a disciplinary penalty for a period not exceeding fifteen days." The court found that the prisoners had been "continuously held in solitary rooms...in violation of the law." The court rejected the authorities' security justifications:

> What has been argued by the administrative authority concerning fears of their escape, in considering them dangerous prisoners, the precedents of the escape of three of their colleagues, and the attacks by some of them on some of the prison guards and workers, is not valid. The administrative authority is capable of undertaking other security measures either inside or outside the prison to prevent their escape or the escape of other prisoners.
>
> In addition, the argument that they were put in solitary rooms as a security measure because there were *occurrences of verbal assaults* by some inmates is not legally allowed.[16]

The court also ruled that the authorities' denial of radios, newspapers and other printed materials to the Jihad prisoners was in violation of the law. This issue is discussed in Chapter Six.

The Jihad prisoners told MEW that following the escape of three of their cellmates in July 1988, their books were confiscated and they were denied the right to take their examinations. Even though these prisoners had been allowed to resume their studies by the time of their interview with MEW, one of them said that in 1991, when he was scheduled to take an examination, he was not allowed to do so, despite permission from the Minister of Interior.

---

[16]Emphasis added.

BEATINGS AND WHIPPINGS:
AUTHORIZED CORPORAL PUNISHMENT

Egyptian law authorizes the beating of juvenile prisoners and the whipping of adult prisoners as a disciplinary penalty.[17] Prisoners under seventeen years old may be beaten ten times with a thin stick, while adult prisoners may receive up to thirty-six lashes with a specially designed whip.[18] In a 1991 report, EOHR described the manner in which a prisoner is whipped:

> The punishment of whipping is applied in all prisons...by tying up the prisoner, half naked to a wooden structure akin to a cross, which jailers have for a great many years given the euphemism *al-arousa* (the bride). The punished prisoner is tied to this structure by the hands and the feet, his face towards it. The lashes then shower upon his back, turning it into a slab of red flesh from which blood flows down [to] the ground under the arousa.[19]

During MEW's visit to Abu Za'bal Liman prison, a faded wooden arousa was in full view, leaning back at a slight angle on a raised cement platform. The frame was shaped like a large "A" with the cross extended. At the ends of the frame were holes through which ties are fastened to bind the victim. Gen. Thabet, the commander of the liman, told MEW that whipping must be authorized by the Prisons Administration in Cairo and is used as a punishment only for major offenses, such as striking a guard or attempting an escape. He said that whipping of a prisoner is

---

[17]Article 43(7) of Law No. 396 of 1956.

[18]The whip used is "made of a conical wood handle 48 cm in length and an inch in diameter, attached on one side to a piece of leather strap connected to a coiled linen rope 35 cm in length, the remainder, being 7 branches, each of which is made of 6 knots, is 50 cm in length are 6 mm in width." EOHR, "Prisons in Egypt: The Model of the Tora Prisons Complex," p. 3.

[19]*Ibid.*, p. 7.

carried out by a soldier under the supervision of an officer[20] and in the presence of a doctor who examines the inmate before the whipping. Gen. Thabet asserted that there were no whippings in 1991 at the liman.

Beating or whipping of prisoners is a clear violation of international law and the Egyptian Constitution. Article 42 of the Constitution prohibits physical or mental harm of prisoners.[21] International standards for the treatment of prisoners categorically prohibit corporal punishment for disciplinary offenses. The International Covenant on Civil and Political Rights and the Convention Against Torture and Other Cruel, Inhuman or Degrading Treatment or Punishment, which Egypt has ratified, also prohibit torture or cruel, inhuman and degrading treatment or punishment.

UNAUTHORIZED PHYSICAL ABUSE

Although Middle East Watch found no evidence that torture or the most severe forms of physical abuse are systematically used within Egypt's prison system, we did find many torture victims among the security prisoners held in two Egyptian prisons, Tora Istikbal and Abu Za'bal Liman. As we documented in a report published in July 1992, security detainees as a matter of practice are either tortured during

---

[20]The physical technique used to administer whipping is important, MEW learned. One Jihad prisoner told MEW that in April 1990, an officer at Tora Liman shouted religious insults. "We began to bang on the bars of our cells, to protest. They took four of us to the arousa. One of us was whipped so hard with eighteen lashes that the arousa was about to fall over." The prisoner explained that there are very specific instructions concerning how the arm should be held when lashes are delivered, with the whip being tightly controlled at the wrist. In this case, the soldier "used broad strokes," extending his entire arm as he threw the whip.

[21]Article 42 provides in pertinent part: "Any person arrested, detained or his freedom restricted shall be treated in the manner concomitant with the preservation of his dignity. No physical or moral harm shall be inflicted on him."

interrogation by SSI prior to their transfer to prison, or are secretly removed from prisons to be tortured in SSI offices.[22]

In addition, inmates are not free from abuse within the walls of a prison. MEW collected information, including personal testimony from victims and eyewitnesses, about incidents of beating, whipping and other physical abuse of male inmates—security and criminal prisoners alike—in 1989, 1990 and 1991. (During our inspections of two prisons where women were held, MEW received no testimony from prisoners about physical abuse.) While it is impossible for MEW to make a definitive judgment about the frequency of such incidents throughout Egypt's prison system, it is clear that male detainees and sentenced prisoners have suffered physical abuse at the hands of prison guards and soldiers, sometimes in the presence of officers. Moreover, in a number of cases, it appears that the infliction of this physical abuse was premeditated and organized.

● A former security prisoner from Cairo, held without charge at Tora Istikbal from February 1991 to January 1992, noted the use of random violence against detainees. "Every three or four days, they would bring Central Security Forces soldiers for the 'prison search.' They would remove our blankets and clothes and beat us with whips." He said that sometimes a liquid would be sprayed into detainees' eyes—"our eyes would swell and we could not see." He also told MEW that detainees were beaten if they asked for medication for medical problems: "You cannot complain. If you do, they hit you."[23]

● An engineer who was held in Tora Istikbal prison after his arrest in April 1989 told MEW that for the first two weeks he was placed in a single cell and never allowed outside. During this time, he witnessed the beating of other prisoners:

> Every two or three days, one of the prisoners was removed from his cell and was violently beaten by about

---

[22]See *Behind Closed Doors* for additional information.

[23]MEW interview, Cairo, February 4, 1992.

twenty soldiers in the hallway. He would be forced to crawl and then was beaten while crawling.

He said that the soldiers typically used sticks and boots to beat the prisoners, but that "sometimes officers had electric sticks." The electric sticks, were about eighteen inches long and over one-inch thick, dark grey in color, and produced a shock when applied to the body.

After the engineer was held for about two weeks, prison officers searched the cells. "I had written some poetry, which they found and confiscated. Then they took me out of the cell, put me in the corridor with another prisoner, and beat us. The other person resisted, and they used a spray on him that burns and blinds the eyes for a half-hour."[24]

● At Abu Za'bal Liman, where some 100 Palestinians were being held without charge or trial under successive detention orders, MEW took testimony about beatings. On July 15, 1991, about nine of the detainees went on a hunger strike to protest their continuous detention without charge and the conditions under which they were being held. "We were taken out separately and beaten with sticks and with hands," one of the strikers said. Then the men were placed for five days in a separate room, and fed only bread. They were never let out of the room, which measured about 6.5-by-6 feet. Some of the detainees developed diarrhea and were denied medical attention.

● A physician who was held in a ground-floor cell at Abu Za'bal Industrial prison in February 1991 told MEW about the use of whips on other detainees by uniformed guards. "An officer with two stars, whose name is known, ordered the whipping. They used leather whips with knots of pieces of metal, on the soles of the feet," he said. "The prisoners were injured, but were forced to run."[25]

● A U.S. citizen witnessed the whipping and beating of new arrivals at Cairo's al-Khalifa prison. He was arrested in Sinai in August 1990 and initially held there in al-Tour prison. He was transferred in the middle

---

[24]MEW interview, Mansoura, February 3, 1992.

[25]MEW interview, New York, December 1991.

of the night of August 29, by truck and then train, to al-Khalifa prison in Cairo. He told MEW that he arrived at al-Khalifa in the late afternoon of August 29:

> I saw the police officers whip several men. The last two men off our truck were Palestinians. I heard screams. The two were beaten with sticks and whips. I saw the welts, the bleeding...it looked like they received a severe beating with wooden sticks. There were at least four police officers beating them. One of the police officers raised his stick and threatened to beat me, but he did not.

> I was taken to a first-floor cell that held forty to fifty men, all of them non-Egyptians. The booking table had a television and a whip, a long bull whip, black or brown. Outside the cell was a Palestinian who was clearly in pain. He had fresh whip marks on his back. He was handcuffed to the bars of the cell, his hands up. He had no shirt and was wearing only shorts.[26]

● A sentenced Islamist prisoner at Tora Liman told MEW that, for the past four years a high-ranking prison officer (whom he named) had been in his present post, he had entered the building housing the Jihad prisoners in the early morning with as many as 200 armed soldiers and up to fifty officers, opening cells randomly and, with pistol drawn, threatened to kill prisoners, saying he had the authority from President Mubarak to kill any or all of the Jihad prisoners. The prisoner said that when one of his cellmates challenged the officer's behavior, he was taken away and returned after being severely beaten.

● Sentenced "Jihad" prisoners complained to MEW about several incidents of whipping at Tora Liman prison. One incident was followed by retaliatory punishment of prisoners who wrote a letter of complaint to President Mubarak. Prisoners said that Ali Ahmed Abdel Monim was taken in the summer of 1989 to the arousa and whipped, for "opposing the insults of the prison director" at that time. Ali had a confrontation

---

[26]MEW interview, New York, June 11, 1991.

with the prison director in the late spring of that year, which led to his confinement with four others in the punishment cells. They were held there for two months, deprived of all clothes, and never let out. After they were returned to the regular cells, Ali was taken out and whipped in the presence of his cellmates. He was given no notice or warning and did not receive a doctor's examination before or after the whipping.

Assam Derbala told MEW that he wrote a letter to President Mubarak in August 1989 to complain about Ali's whipping. In the letter, he outlined the prisoners' version of the events and complained about "psychological torture." He sent the letter "through the normal channels" and was surprised four days later when prison security officers searched his cell and the cell of another inmate, Assam Abdel Magid Muhammed Naji. According to Assam, both men were beaten on sensitive parts of their bodies, their clothes were taken and shredded, and they were placed in the punishment cells. Assam said that they were told that they were being punished because of the letter, and that they would learn not to talk again. Four times since this incident, he contends, prison security officers have come by and said, "Get ready, your time is coming."

● As discussed earlier in this chapter, inmates sometimes are beaten inside punishment wings. At Tora Liman, MEW interviewed one prisoner in a punishment cell who said that inmates in the punishment wing "sometimes are beaten, and guards put shoes in their mouths" so the sound will not carry. He pointed to Cell Thirteen and said: "The guy in there was just beaten yesterday for one hour." He also said that the prisoner in Cell Fifteen had received thirty-six lashes on his back on January 16, 1991.

● Some of the most vulnerable inmates in Egypt's penal institutions are foreign prisoners, often men and women from other African countries. MEW received a letter from one foreign prisoner, dated April 1, 1992, who had been held at Abu Za'bal Liman prison but at the time of writing the letter was being held at another facility. He described the beating of several foreign prisoners, and asserted that in two cases the prisoners had died from their injuries:

> [At Abu Za'bal] the warders constantly kick, slap, box, and whip the prisoners for slight disagreements with them before sending on to [the] Black Room. In the

Black Room one is whipped every morning by a soldier specially trained for whipping. The number of lashes depends on the discretion of the one who is in charge of the Black Room. One [Saudi Arabian] by the name [Mansour] Salah Musalhi committed suicide after a severe beating by one of the warders in January 1988...

[At Qanater] Mr. Talip Kilich (from Turkey, 52 years) died in his room after he was beaten by jail warders on July 27, 1991. Mohammed Mahmud Shak (a Somali) died on [November 29, 1991]. He was severely beaten after he attempted to escape. Despite the seventy-five lashes authorized (with hands, legs, and head tied on a wood shaped like a cross) about one hundred warders took their turn of beating him. He was later transferred to the underground cell where he died. He was not given any treatment for the wounds he sustained from beating and no food was given to him.

Joseph Author (34 years, from Ghana) was beaten severely [on February 2, 1992] by the warders, for the fault of somebody else. This sparked off an angry protest by all the foreigners in Qanater prison. Later the manager came and promised him medical treatment just to calm down the angry foreigners, but he was never given any treatment. The doctor prescribed medicines but since Joe didn't have the money to buy them, he was left to suffer the panel [sic] beating without medical attention.

In October 1992, Middle East Watch wrote to Interior Minister Gen. Abdel Halim Moussa and Prosecutor General Raga el-Araby about the alleged deaths of Kilich and Shak, and requested information about their cases. As of this writing, MEW has not received a reply from either official.

In November 1992, Middle East Watch received a letter from a sentenced inmate at Qanater men's prison, in which he described the mistreatment and beating of foreign prisoners held in three cells in Building B of the facility. According to the prisoner's account, on

September 6, 1992, Cells 5/6, I/7 and 4/7—all of them holding foreign nationals—were ransacked by guards. Prisoners' pots, spoons, plates, stoves, buckets, water-storage cans, towels, clothing and bedsheets were confiscated. The shelves in the cells were broken. To thwart imminent protest about this treatment, anti-riot forces were called in and the prisoners were beaten.

Prior to the beatings, the prisoners in the three cells who were of British and Spanish nationality were removed, leaving only the prisoners from non-Western countries. Several days later, the occupants of Cell 5/6 asked one of the prison officials to explain the reasons for the abuse. In response, he confined them to their cell for forty-eight hours, the door locked shut. On November 20, 1992, Middle East Watch reported this incident to Prosecutor General el-Araby. We asked that his office investigate the complaint[27] and provide Middle East Watch with a copy of the results of the investigation. As of this writing, we have not received an acknowledgement of this letter from the Prosecutor General, nor any information from his office about the status of the investigation.

THE "BEATING FORCE"

MEW found substantial evidence that at least some of the beatings have been highly organized, involving large numbers of soldiers. Former prisoners, in separate interviews, provided testimony about a "beating force" used to inflict physical abuse on security detainees in Tora and Abu Za'bal prisons. Their accounts indicate that this "beating force" has been in operation at least since 1989 and has been used against both Islamist and secular security detainees:

● A university student from Assyut, who was held without charge at Tora Istikbal prison from October 1991 until his release in December 1991, told MEW that he was mistreated once while at the prison:

---

[27]At a meeting with Middle East Watch representatives in February 1992, Chancellor el-Araby stated that there is an immediate visit by a district niyaba following the receipt of a complaint by the prosecutor general.

I was beaten once. I was taken out into the big hall and about forty soldiers encircled me. I turned and they hit me with electric sticks. The sticks were about forty to fifty centimeters long [16 to 20 inches], black with plastic. It lasted for about ten minutes. They hit me on the head and I collapsed. This group is called "the beating force."[28]

● Another former security detainee told MEW about his treatment by prison guards when he arrived at Tora Istikbal in March 1991, after eighteen days of detention and torture at an "unknown location." He said that after his arrival at the prison, his head was shaven. Then he was brought to the holding area, where there was a line of Central Security Forces soldiers. He and the other detainees were forced to walk down the line, past the soldiers. "Each one takes a punch at you," he said. Because he was weak from torture that he claimed he had been subjected to immediately prior to his transfer to Tora Istikbal, he fainted from the first punch. When he awoke, he was moved into solitary confinement and held there for eighteen days.[29]

● On August 8, 1989, trade unionist Mustafa Naib was transferred to Tora prison, where he encountered a special "reception." Two lines of Central Security Forces soldiers formed a corridor and beat Naib and other newly arrived detainees with sticks as they moved from the vehicle that had transported them into the prison.[30]

● EOHR also described such a "beating force" at Abu Za'bal Liman prison, where an EOHR lawyer and two members of its board of directors—one of them a lawyer—were beaten in August 1989:

> Beating often takes place following group arrests directly on arrival at the prison or shortly thereafter, in the form of what has become termed as *tashrifa*, or reception ceremony. This has become one of the rites greeting

---

[28]MEW interview, Assyut, February 10, 1992.

[29]MEW interview, Cairo, February 4, 1992.

[30]Interview by Dr. Robert S. Lawrence, Cairo, May 26, 1990.

political prisoners on their arrival in prison and to which two members of EOHR's board of trustees (Dr. Mohammed As-Sayyid Said and Amir Salem) were subjected, together with a number of others arrested at the same time for their alleged membership of the Egyptian Workers' Communist Party. As a result, a number of them sustained serious injuries from the severity of the beatings and from being dragged along the floor of the prison.

Hisham Mubarak, a lawyer, suffered a hemorrhage in his right ear and (temporary) loss of hearing, in addition to scars on his back and on the back of his head. He was unable to move his right leg as a result of blows directed at his spine. Kamal Khalil, an engineer, suffered from severe depression and bruising of the shoulders and buttocks, as well as fractured ribs caused by beatings with sticks and an electric baton, slaps and kicks and an officer jumping on his back for several minutes as he lay sprawled in his cell.[31]

● The most detailed testimony about organized violence in a prison was taken by a participant in the Middle East Watch fact-finding mission to Egypt in 1990. This member of the delegation, a physician, interviewed Kamal Khalil, the engineer noted in the paragraph above. Khalil was arrested on August 24, 1989, accused of membership in the Workers' Communist Party. He suffered serious injuries during incidents of organized violence by soldiers and officers at Abu Za'bal prison. He was released on September 7, 1989.

Khalil was transferred to Abu Za'bal on August 28, 1989, when a large van carrying twenty-six men arrived at the police station where he was being held with twenty-six other men. All fifty-two men were

---

[31]EOHR, "Torture in Egypt in 1989," January 1990, p. 4.

manacled and transported to Abu Za'bal Industrial prison. There, they were divided among five cells, about ten men per cell.[32]

At 12:30 a.m., a large group of soldiers[33] arrived outside the cells and began doing calisthenics and drilling, accompanied by loud shouting. This lasted for about one hour. The soldiers then were forced to stand in the corridor outside the cells for the remainder of the night. Khalil believed this was done to make the soldiers resentful of the prisoners and to prepare them for the subsequent abusive behavior.

At 8:00 the next morning, on what is now called "Black Monday" by those who were victimized, Khalil was awakened by a friend who pointed out soldiers in the corridor, some with guns, others with clubs or holding dogs. Suddenly, orders were given for the soldiers to attack the prisoners in Cell One. Khalil was in Cell Five, and for the next several hours he heard the screams as the soldiers spent about one hour with each group of prisoners.

When the police reached his cell, they entered and instructed the prisoners to stand against the wall with their hands above their heads facing the wall. Three of the inmates were identified as "looking like leaders" and were removed. One was Medhat el-Zahed, a journalist. The soldiers then beat the remaining seven prisoners with clubs across the back and on the buttocks; electric shocks were applied to their necks; their heads were grasped and pounded against the wall.

---

[32]Khalil recounted cell conditions that were similar to those described in this report by other former and current prisoners held in the liman at Abu Za'bal. The floor was broken cement, with cracks hiding large numbers of insects. The prisoners also were plagued by large numbers of mosquitoes from the lake. Their request for blankets and bedding was denied. At 11:00 p.m., one of Khalil's cellmates asked a guard to call his officer so they could press their demand for bedding. The officer told them that the Minister of the Interior had given instructions that they should sleep on the bare floor.

[33]The reference here and throughout Khalil's testimony is most likely to Central Security Forces soldiers (see Glossary).

The seven men had committed themselves to silence rather than scream as had the other groups. Their stoicism angered the officer in charge, who commanded the soldiers to drive them out into the corridor where more soldiers were lined up in two rows, forming a gauntlet, about fifty soldiers per row. The seven detainees were driven down the corridor, beaten by the soldiers until they reached the end where the dogs were waiting. They were turned back and were again beaten as they returned toward their cell door. Again, they were lined up against the cell wall with their hands above their heads. Khalil turned his head to face the commanding officer who said, "This son of a dog wants to make a torture accusation."

Five soldiers then seized him, and one beat his head against the wall until he lost consciousness. He had water thrown on him and initially feigned continued unconsciousness, hoping the soldiers would stop beating him and his colleagues. When he saw that the police were continuing to beat the others, he stood to his feet and was again beaten until the commanding officer called a halt. The entire episode lasted about a half hour. The soldiers left the cell and locked the door.

As the seven men sat and examined their wounds, one of them commented that it was his birthday, and they all began joking about his birthday gift, "laughing out of our misery." One of the officers heard them laughing, opened the cell door, and the soldiers returned to beat them for another five minutes. This time they were instructed to lie prone on the cell floor. One of the soldiers pointed to Khalil and said that he was the one who had demanded proper bedding the previous day. The officer, Mustafa el-Nadim, said, "I'll get you a nice bed," and started jumping on Khalil's back with his heavy boots for almost five minutes. The soldiers then left.

Medical Care Denied: Khalil believes that the soldiers were trained to hurt them but not to kill them because, throughout the beatings, the soldiers avoided hitting them over the kidneys. Khalil was unable to walk and feared that he had suffered internal bleeding. Mohamed Husseini Shamaa was also badly injured with a bleeding neck wound. They asked to be seen by the prison doctor, but when they were taken to the doctor, they found the commander of the soldiers, Mohamed Salah, sitting next to the doctor. The doctor refused to examine them or to give them any medications.

A Complaint to the Niyaba and More Punishment: Two days later, when Khalil was taken for his deposition, he told the niyaba the story of his torture and that he had been threatened that he would be tortured further if he described his experience to anyone. The prosecutor observed the bruises on Khalil's body and entered the description into the deposition. Khalil was returned to prison but—because of his complaint, he believed—he was placed in a cell with worse conditions—it was totally dark, filled with roaches, had no drinking water, and sewage flooded the floor. His food was confiscated. Khalil remained in these circumstances from 10:00 p.m. until 4:00 p.m. the following day.

He started to vomit and asked for water. An officer removed him from the cell, pointed to a nearby refuse heap and instructed him to find two bottles, one for drinking water and one for a urinal. He was then allowed about five minutes to fill one of the bottles with water and to take some prison food which he described as "rotten beans." He refused to return to the cell. He told the officer to examine the cell and warned that he would be responsible in the case of his death.

Transfer to the Prison Hospital: At this point, the officer took Khalil to the prison hospital. No treatment was provided, but the prison director did give him permission to remain in the hospital and sleep in a bed rather than return to his cell, "since there are no medications." He remained in the hospital for another three days.

Release from Prison and Surgery: Khalil was then brought for a forensic medical examination; the doctor found sufficient evidence to declare that he had been tortured. After another two days in the prison hospital, he was again brought before the niyaba. A decision to release him was made on September 5, 1989, in response to international pressure. He was finally released on September 7 and went directly to the Ibn Sinna Hospital. On September 12, surgery was performed to drain a large hematoma from his right buttock; about 1.5 liters of clotted blood were evacuated. His chest was taped to aid in the healing of bruised ribs from the stomping he had received.[34]

---

[34]Interview by Dr. Robert S. Lawrence, Cairo, May 26, 1990.

5
MEDICAL SERVICES AND FACILITIES

*"I was in serious pain from influenza and kidney problems,
but I never saw a doctor or a nurse. They are ghosts."*

> *— Sixty-year-old Egyptian security detainee held in
> Abu Za'bal prison following his October 1991
> arrest.*

*"I come from a poor family....I'm suffering from chest pain
and sometimes when I cough I spit blood. Here there's not
any treatment. The doctor simply told me to buy the
medicine [at] my own expense. What I'm trying to tell you
is: my life is in danger if I do not get the right medicine
soon."*

> *— African prisoner held in Zaqaziq prison, writing
> to MEW in a letter dated October 23, 1992.*

MEW heard numerous complaints about medical services from
former and current prisoners, despite the fact that the Prisons
Administration claims that health care is "at the forefront" of the various
"humanitarian programs" in Egypt's prison system.[1] The most serious
complaints concerned the denial of medical attention to prisoners who
urgently required care or who had been recommended for specialized
treatment in outside hospitals. Some prisoners mentioned the names of
individuals who had died in prison hospitals or in their cells, allegedly
because of poor or nonexistent medical care. MEW also took complaints
from prisoners who said that they were ill and had been denied requests
to be examined by prison doctors, saw the prison doctor but received only
superficial examinations, or were provided only aspirin as medicine for
various medical problems. Inmates said that prison doctors only provided
prescriptions for medication, and that the prisoners themselves, or their
families, had to pay for the drugs. These practices are breaches of

---

[1]Statement given to MEW representatives by Prisons Administration director,
General Fakarani, February 20, 1992.

international standards, which require daily medical supervision of prisoners who are sick or who complain of illness.[2]

Dr. Sayyid Awad Sayyid, the general medical director of the Prisons Administration, denied that there are any problems with regard to medical services and care. "There are no problems from the medical point of view," he told MEW. "Every prisoner receives all his rights regarding medical care, prophylaxis and treatment."[3] Dr. Sayyid stressed that the prisons' medical staffs are adequate: "In every prison, there are one or two or three doctors. If a prisoner wants a doctor, he'll find one. There are doctors at night for necessary cases." Dr. Sayyid dismissed prisoners' complaints as lies. "Most prisoners want to be free. They say medical treatment is bad, nourishment is inadequate and that they are punished. They are liars."

Physicians who have been held in Egyptian prisons, as well as other former and current prisoners, disputed Dr. Sayyid's assertions. An Egyptian urologic surgeon, sixty-seven years old at the time of his interview in 1990, had been held in five different prisons after his arrest in August 1989. He said that while in prison he tried but was unable to provide medical care to fellow inmates because he lacked equipment. He said that no medical care was provided by the prison authorities, and cited the case of one man who suffered from severe renal colic and was unable to obtain even an aspirin for his pain.[4]

---

[2]Article 25(1) of the United Nations Minimum Rules specifies: "The medical officer shall have the care of the physical and mental health of the prisoners and should daily see all sick prisoners, all who complain of illness, and any prisoner to whom his attention is specially directed."

[3]MEW interview, Cairo, February 20, 1992.

[4]Interview by Dr. Robert S. Lawrence, Cairo, May 28, 1990.

PRISONERS' COMPLAINTS ABOUT MEDICAL SERVICES

Officials told MEW that all but two or three of Egypt's thirty prisons have a hospital, and that every prison has a medical staff, with the size dependent on the inmate population. According to information supplied to MEW by the Prisons Administration, prison hospitals are staffed by thirty-seven doctors employed by the Prisons Administration and fifty-two physicians from the Ministry of Health. In the three-month period from July 1 to September 30, 1991, the Prisons Administration reported that 4,692 prisoners were treated for emergency conditions. Prison doctors told MEW that among the most common medical problems in the prison system were scabies, various skin diseases, influenza and the common cold, diarrhea and rheumatic pains.[5] One physician who was serving his tenth year at Tora Liman told MEW that bronchitis, asthma, rheumatic pains, depression and hysterical fits were common medical problems of many Islamist prisoners. He also noted that some prisoners in their thirties and forties have developed angina, a disease more typically found in older people.[6] He added that the "continuous tension" in the prison contributed to poor health.

During MEW's brief visit to Tora Istikbal, where approximately 400 security prisoners were on hunger strike, detainees provided a seven-page handwritten list that contained the names of 202 of the security prisoners with a variety of information about them, including medical problems they said that they suffered. Fifteeen (seven percent) reported kidney and/or urinary troubles; eight (four percent) suffered from skin diseases, six from piles or fissures, five from undifferentiated convulsions,

---

[5]The medical director of Abu Za'bal Liman hospital told MEW that there were no deaths in the prison in 1991. He said that there were four deaths in 1990: three prisoners died in the prison—from heart failure, tuberculosis, and liver failure, respectively; the fourth died in an outside hospital from a brain tumor.

[6]The dictionary definition of angina pectoris is "severe paroxysmal pain in the chest, associated with emotional stress and characterized by feelings of suffocation and apprehension."

three from nervous breakdown, two with asthmatic chest, one with urinary incontinence and another with gastric ulcer.[7]

MEW found that the adequacy of medical services varies from prison to prison. We took numerous complaints about poor medical services from former and current prisoners at Abu Za'bal Liman, Tora Liman, Tora Istikbal and Tora Mazraa. In contrast, random interviews with men at Tanta general prison yielded no major complaints about medical services or care. (See Chapter Eight for information about medical services and facilities for women prisoners.)

Delays in Providing Emergency Medical Care

Prisoners at Tora Mazraa complained that doctors and nurses were not at the prison around-the-clock, leaving inmates vulnerable in the event of a crisis requiring immediate medical intervention. They said that several weeks before MEW's visit—around February 4, 1992—a prisoner had died in Wing Four, with no doctor coming to his assistance between the time he was taken ill at 11:00 p.m. until he died three hours later.

The prisoner's name was Ibrahim Tantawi. He was approximately sixty years old and was serving a twenty-year narcotics sentence. Inmates said that Tantawi had served over nineteen years and that his sentence was due to expire thirty days after the date of his death. According to the inmates, Tantawi had a cardiac condition, and had been sent for treatment at Cairo University hospital. On the night of his death, at about 11 p.m., he had fallen ill. Fellow inmates banged on the doors of their cells, calling for help. Although a guard did appear, and reportedly informed an officer, inmates said that no doctor came to Tantawi's cell. He died in Wing Four at approximately 2:00 a.m.

---

[7]Other reported medical problems were most probably chronic and irrelevant to their situation as a primary cause, according to an Egyptian physician who analyzed the data provided by the detainees. These problems included anemia, cardiovascular disorders, chronic gastro-intestinal troubles and rheumatic affliction.

In October 1992, MEW wrote to Egypt's Interior Minister and Prosecutor General, requesting information about the Tantawi case. As of this writing, there has been no reply from either of these officials.

In August 1991, EOHR reported the case of Shehata Abdel Hamid, a sixty-three-year-old worker who died immediately after release from Tora Istikbal. According to EOHR, Shehata, who had been detained on May 28, 1989, began "to suffer from continuous vomiting and very high blood pressure" in late July of that year, by which time he was already incapable of walking or standing. Days later, following an incident where his cellmates were forced to stand him up for an inspection by the director of the prison, he suffered kidney failure. Even after a prison medical officer ordered that Shehata be transferred to a hospital, he was reportedly held several days and then released, brought by prison officials to his home and not a hospital. Two days later, Shehata died in a hospital to which his family had taken him.[8]

Denial of Specialized Medical Treatment at Outside Hospitals

The medical director of the Prisons Administration, Dr. Sayyid, told MEW that most surgical operations are performed at prison hospitals, with the exception of cases requiring special skills or treatment. Such cases are transferred to university hospitals. He emphasized that any medical service needed by prisoners that cannot be accommodated within the prison medical system will be secured from outside specialists and hospitals.[9] He noted, for example, that prisoners with kidney failure are treated at specialized medical centers in Cairo, often three times a week, and that the Prisons Administration bears the cost of this treatment. Dr. Sayyid also said that prisoners who suffer from serious illnesses, such as cancer and kidney disease, are examined by a committee

---

[8]EOHR, "Prisons in Egypt: The Model of the Tora Prisons Complex," p. 11.

[9]He cited the case of a prisoner at Tora Liman who needed an operation for the removal of his gall bladder. The surgeon at the prison hospital could not perform the operation. Specialists were identified from a university hospital to perform the operation but the patient, Muhammed Ali Berro, a Lebanese serving a sentence for narcotics, refused because he was afraid of having an operation.

consisting of a doctor from outside the prison and the medical director of the specific prison. If this committee finds that the prisoner's continued stay in prison exposes his life to danger, he is released, according to Dr. Sayyid. The doctor further said: "In this month alone [February 1992] we have set free six prisoners: three cancer cases, one heart failure case, and two cases of renal [kidney] failure."[10]

Despite these assurances, MEW gathered information about cases in which prisoners were denied specialized medical treatment outside the prison. Security prisoners appear to have particular difficulty in securing permission for treatment at outside hospitals. Numerous prisoners mentioned to MEW that permission is needed from SSI before any security prisoner—sentenced or detained without charge—can be moved into a prison hospital or to an outside medical facility. These prisoners further asserted that SSI often denies inmates access to outside hospitals. Such practices violate international standards.[11]

• Inmates at Tora Mazraa brought MEW representatives to one sentenced prisoner with a disfiguring skin disease, consisting of numerous small hard lumps that covered the entire surface of his face. He recently had been denied specialized medical care that was recommended by an independent dermatological specialist. According to the prisoner, three-and-a-half years earlier he had been examined by Dr. Muhammed Abdallah Rahim, the head of dermatology at the Ain Shams medical faculty, and treated there. His condition worsened and he sought to return to Ain Shams. On January 7, 1992, Dr. Abdallah Rahim recommended that the prisoner be admitted to Ain Shams the next day for in-patient treatment. The prisoner spent one month attempting to secure permission to go to the hospital.

---

[10]The committee's decision to release is not final, however. It must be approved, according to General Fakarani, by the General Prosecutor after it is reviewed by the Director of the Prisons Administration, Fakarani himself. Only after both approve is the prisoner released. MEW interview, Cairo, February 20, 1992.

[11]Article 22(2) of the United Nations Minimum Rules provides in pertinent part: "Sick prisoners who require specialist treatment shall be transferred to specialized institutions or to civil hospitals."

On February 4—two weeks before his interview with MEW—he was brought by car to Ain Shams, accompanied by prison guards. The prisoner carried a letter of permission from Dr. Sayyid Awad Sayyid, the medical director of the Prisons Administration. The prisoner understood that he was to be admitted to the in-patient clinic but instead was driven to the outpatient clinic. He told MEW that he sat outside in the car for two to three hours and then was returned to Tora Mazraa. On February 5, the prisoner complained directly to Dr. Sayyid, who promised him that he would be returned to Ain Shams. "Since this time," the prisoner said, "I learned that there is a letter in my file that says my case is not urgent and that I must be treated at Tora Mazraa hospital."

● Sentenced "Jihad" prisoners at Tora Liman also complained about the denial of specialized medical treatment for inmates with serious medical problems. Nabil el-Magraby, for example, said that he was suffering from peptic ulcer, water in the lungs, cardiac problems and edema.[12] He showed MEW his grossly swollen and purplish-red legs. "A doctor saw my legs four months ago at Kasr el-Aini hospital. The doctor wanted me to be treated at the hospital, but SSI would not allow it." Magraby said that he receives some medicine for his ailments from his family but "other medicines are not allowed in." He said that he needs medicine for his ulcer and for angina.

Another sentenced Jihad prisoner, thirty-five-year-old Ghadban Ali Said, who had been imprisoned since 1981, has epilepsy. Fellow prisoners told MEW that he suffers seizures and loses consciousness.

---

[12]Maghraby had difficulty for some time in obtaining treatment for his medical problems. In June 1990, EOHR issued two urgent appeals on his behalf. The first appeal, dated June 4, EOHR criticized Maghraby's "lack of necessary medical care and nutrition" at the Tora prison hospital. The second appeal, dated June 28, stated that EOHR had received a copy of official medical reports for Maghraby, which confirmed that he was suffering from coronary cycle deficiency, coronary thrombosis, severe albumin deficiency because of poor nutrition and an ulcer, among other illnesses. EOHR further noted that one of the medical reports, which was dated February 13, 1990, contained a recommendation from the prison doctor that Maghraby be immediately transferred to al-Manial University Hospital.

They claimed that he is not properly treated at the prison and needs an electro-encephalograph (EEG).

Denial of Medical Care at Prison Hospitals

MEW took testimony from current and former prisoners who claimed that medical care and treatment had been denied to prisoners who were ill. MEW also received information suggesting that at some prisons it was necessary to bribe staff to obtain admission to the hospital. At Tora Mazraa, several prisoners told MEW that inmates needed to bribe prison personnel to obtain services. "It costs LE 20 (about six dollars) for an evaluation, and more money to actually get admitted to the hospital," one said. In a separate interview, another prisoner told MEW: "To go to the hospital, you have to pay." The relative of a U.S. citizen imprisoned at Qanater women's prison told MEW that her sister has been unsuccessful in gaining admission to the prison hospital for treatment of scabies; the relative, who lives in Cairo, said that she believes she needs to pay money to a specific doctor to secure her sister's transfer to the hospital.[13]

● Dr. Sayyid Muhammed Abdul, who has been the medical director at Abu Za'bal Liman since 1967, said that some 100 patients are seen daily by the medical staff. He indicated that it was easy for any inmate to secure medical attention. Once the director of a cell block is notified, the inmate is brought to the clinic. In addition, he said, "every week the doctors inspect all the cells." But Palestinian long-term security prisoners in the liman brought up case after case in which medical care had not been provided to prisoners who were ill.

The prisoners brought MEW representatives to Ahmad el-Kourdi, a man in his late fifties who said he had been arrested at his home in Sinai on October 8, 1990 and transferred to the liman on October 17, 1990. He could no longer see from his left eye; he said that he lost his vision three months prior to MEW's visit. "And my right eye is bad," he said. "I have not seen a doctor. I have asked at least three times." In an August 1992 letter to MEW, the Palestinian prisoners wrote that al-Kourdi "needs urgent surgery, according to the report of a specialist

---

[13]MEW telephone interview, October 6, 1992.

physician. But the security [sic] refused to give permission for shifting him to hospital to do the surgery."[14]

Abdel Nasser Bilal, a bespectacled twenty-eight-year-old university student detained without charge since his arrest in September 1990, told MEW that before his transfer to Abu Za'bal Liman, he had been held incommunicado, continuously blindfolded, in the SSI office in Alexandria. The blindfolding for almost three weeks caused severe eye problems, for which he said that he had been unable to secure treatment:

> I used to suffer from some problems in my eyes, for which I wore contact lenses. At the SSI office, they tied my eyes with a tight blindfold for twenty days, on top of my lenses, which should have been removed. This caused infection and swelling in my eyes. Then I was brought to Abu Za'bal and my condition started to deteriorate, until I lost sight in my right eye. Now I am about to lose sight in my left eye. The director of the prison hospital suggested my transfer to Tora prison hospital. He contacted SSI, but they said no.[15]

(Eye care was also noted as a problem by prisoners at Tora Liman. Eight sentenced security prisoners who wear eyeglasses said that they receive

---

[14]Letter to MEW from "Arrested Palestinian People in Abu Za'bal Jail," dated August 22, 1992.

[15]When MEW representatives met with Dr. Sayyid, the medical director of the Prisons Administration, we discussed Bilal's case. Dr. Sayyid left the room and returned with two short handwritten letters. The first, dated February 16 (with no year provided), from the prisoner affairs department to Dr. Sayyid, referred to a letter written by Dr. Sayyid dated February 10 regarding the transfer of Bilal to Tora Liman hospital because "he suffers from severe loss of vision." The letter noted that Bilal had not yet been transferred. In a reply dated February 20, Dr. Sayyid wrote that there was no objection to transferring Bilal to Qanater prison hospital for examination on February 24, 1992. MEW met with Bilal on February 12, 1992 and took his testimony; the meeting with Dr. Sayyid was on February 20, 1992.

no eye examinations and had been asking for a year to see an eye doctor.)

In the same cell with Bilal, other prisoners said that they were suffering from untreated medical problems, including asthma, cardiac problems and rheumatism. One detainee had bullet fragments in his right thigh that sometimes produced pain so intense he was unable to walk; he said that his request to be sent to hospital for treatment had been refused.

● In one cell on the first floor of Building A at Tora Istikbal, inmates—speaking to a MEW representative through a window above their locked door—said that Hussein Muhammed Hussein could not get up and his kidneys "were not functioning." They told MEW: "We have been screaming for a doctor for eight days." The men had been held inside this cell for two months without ever being let outside.

Later, another MEW representative visited the cell, saw Hussein and obtained additional information. Hussein, who appeared quite ill, was unable to sit up or talk. His cellmates said that he was a diabetic and had been held at Tora Istikbal for seven months. According to his cellmates, he had taken very ill three days before, at which point they called for the prison doctor who, they claimed, refused to treat Hussein "as long as he is on strike." MEW was unable to determine whether Hussein was in fact a participant in the hunger strike. MEW did find, minutes later at the conclusion of its inspection, that two other inmates, both strikers, were being treated while Hussein remained in his cell unattended, suggesting an arbitrariness in provision of medical services.

● A Muslim Brotherhood leader from Alexandria was arrested in October 1991 and held without charge at Abu Za'bal for two months. "There was no medical attention," he charged. He said that he asked frequently for medical assistance. "I was in serious pain from influenza and kidney problems, but I never saw a doctor or a nurse. They are ghosts."[16] Another Muslim Brotherhood activist who was arrested at the same time and also held in Abu Za'bal told MEW that "no doctors or nurses" were made available to prisoners who were ill. He noted that one

---

[16]MEW interview, Alexandria, February 1, 1992.

of his cellmates had an abscess on his arm and had been unable to secure medical attention. A fellow cellmate, who was a doctor, lanced the abscess in the cell.[17]

● A fourth-year student at the University of Assyut was arrested in October 1991 and, after one month at the general prison in Assyut, was transferred to Tora Istikbal. He was held in a small ground-floor cell with only one blanket to serve as a mattress and a cover. For the first thirty days, he was permitted no visits from his family or lawyer. He developed diarrhea and tonsilitis from the cold. "I was never let out of my cell," he told MEW. "I asked to go to the clinic but I was refused. If you are ill and knock on the cell door, the guard comes and threatens to beat you."[18]

Prisoners also complained that their admission to prison hospitals was delayed, sometimes for days. On the first floor of the hospital at Tora Mazraa, MEW found three patients who did not have beds and were sleeping on the floor on thin, prison-issue grey blankets. One of them, who had been in the hospital for two weeks and was sleeping on two thin blankets, said he had heart problems. He said that he had experienced spasms and weakness of breath but was forced to wait three days before he was examined by a doctor and transferred to the hospital.

Limited Availability of Medicines

The most common complaint MEW heard from prisoners concerned the lack of medicines other than aspirin, despite the authorities' claim that all prisons were supplied with all the necessary medicines.[19] One of the very first prisoners MEW interviewed, at Abu

---

[17]Ibid.

[18]MEW interview, Assyut, February 10, 1992.

[19]According to the Prisons Administration, all Egyptian prisons "contain pharmacies that have necessary medicines, which are supplied regularly with what they needed from the pharmaceutical division in the department, for which appropriate annual funds are designated." (Statement given to MEW

Za'bal Liman, said that inmates were given "aspirin only." He insisted that no other medicines were provided. A medical doctor, held for twenty-two days beginning November 22, 1991, also claimed that "there are no medicines at Tora Istikbal—only aspirin."[20] We continued to hear this complaint throughout the prison system.

When prescriptions are given by prison doctors, inmates say that they are required to purchase the medicine with their own money. Numerous prisoners said that prescription drugs were brought to them by their families. In Abu Za'bal Liman, MEW met a forty-seven-year-old prisoner who said that he suffered from high blood pressure. He said that he requires Brinerdin/Sandoz for medication but it was not provided by the prison hospital; rather, his family brings him the medication on a regular basis. A twenty-year-old asthmatic, in a separate interview, said that his family provides him with the medicine he needs. A sixty-year-old prisoner, who has been at Abu Za'bal for two years serving a ten-year sentence, told MEW that he suffered from rheumatic pains in his legs from the cold (he was shaking and trembling during the interview). "All I get is two capsules from the doctor. If you have money, then you can bring medicine from the outside," he said.

This system imposes potentially life-threatening hardships on impoverished prisoners and foreign-national prisoners whose families are unable to visit them or to send money. One African prisoner held at Zaqaziq prison wrote to MEW in a letter dated October 23, 1992 that he was "suffering from chest pain and sometimes when I cough I spit blood. Here, there's not any treatment. The doctor simply told me to buy the

---

representatives by Gen. Fakarani, director of the Prisons Administration, on February 20, 1992.) In addition, Dr. Sayyid Awad Sayyid, the medical director of the Prisons Administration, told MEW that the Prisons Administration makes special efforts to locate medicines needed for certain patients if these drugs are not available in the prisons or "even in the market," searching until the drug or a substitute can be found. Dr. Sayyid said that the Prisons Administration "insists on this because any patient outside can search for drugs by himself but the prisoner is our responsibility and cannot search for his treatment." (MEW interview, Cairo, February 20, 1992.)

[20]MEW interview Cairo, January 30, 1992.

medicine [at] my own expense." Explaining that his family is poor, living in a distant African country and unable to help him, the prisoner stated: "What I'm trying to tell you is: my life is in danger if I do not get the right medicine soon....Please, if you can arrange for me some medicines for bronchitis and send them to me...that would be a great thing."

"One is made to buy the medicines prescribed by the doctor," an African prisoner who has been held at four different Egyptian prisons wrote in a letter to MEW. While he was held at Abu Za'bal Liman, he noted the following:

> One Mr. Ram Singh (Indian, sixty years old) died on January 30, 1988 due to lack of medicine. He was suffering from diabetes and had no money to buy medicines prescribed by the doctor.[21]

Handicapped Prisoners

Egyptian prisons lack special accommodations for handicapped prisoners, including blind prisoners. In a cell visited at random in the First Department of Abu Za'bal Liman, MEW found Salah Salam Salam in an overcrowded second-floor cell. Salah is serving a twenty-five-year narcotics sentence, according to a cellmate. Salah is only about two feet tall, and his arms and legs are severely underdeveloped and apparently not very useful. One cellmate explained that Salah "cannot do anything for himself." He said that he and the other cellmates bathed, fed and otherwise cared for Salah, and that the prison authorities provided Salah with no special assistance or accommodations.

At Tora Mazraa, MEW found several blind prisoners. MEW interviewed a young prisoner serving a sentence for theft who claimed that he was completely blind[22]—and certainly appeared to suffer from

---

[21] Letter to MEW, dated April 1, 1992.

[22] Apparently a professional pickpocket with previous arrests, the prisoner said his blindness was a result of torture at a police station, where he was struck on the head and neck with gun butts. He told MEW that he suffered retinal

major sight impairment—but that he had never been seen by a doctor at the prison and that his file had no notation that he was blind.

In one group cell at Tora Mazraa, MEW found a seventy-three-year-old inmate who was serving a five-year sentence for buying stolen goods. He is completely blind and, according to fellow inmates, cannot care for himself. "Prisoners in this cell clean him, feed him and take him to the toilet. He is a problem for the other inmates because he wets himself," one cellmate told MEW. In the prison hospital, there were at least four other inmates who were at least partially blind. None of these inmates received special services to accommodate their handicap and were forced to rely on the benevolence of fellow inmates for everyday survival.

As discussed above, prison medical practices may be increasing the number of blind prisoners. MEW received several complaints about prisoners who were losing their sight but had been denied requests for specialized medical care.

PHYSICAL CONDITIONS IN HOSPITALS

Of the six prisons MEW visited, only four—Abu Za'bal Liman, Tora Liman, Tanta, and Qanater women's prisons—had hospital facilities. Tora Istikbal and Tora Mazraa rely on Tora Liman prison hospital and only have "clinics" to pre-screen inmates and hold prisoners who are ill until they are transferred to the hospital at the Liman.

Filth and poor sanitary conditions prevailed in the prison hospital wards and bathrooms inspected by MEW. Some wards were severely overcrowded, with some prisoners in beds but others sleeping on thin blankets on the floor. Other sections of hospitals that MEW inspected gave the appearance of not having been used in some time: objects were covered with thick layers of dust and furniture was arranged haphazardly, often pushed off to the sides or back of the rooms; in some cases, supplies and equipment were not in obvious view.

---

detachment from these beatings and had been treated, unsuccessfully, at Cairo University hospital.

Patients' Wards

The ward at the prison hospital at Abu Za'bal Liman was grossly unsanitary when MEW visited. There were twelve beds, some of which were covered with dirty sheets and blankets, which the patients apparently provided themselves. Around the beds were the patient's possessions, including water bottles, food (in some cases uncovered and spilling onto the floor), boxes with other personal articles, and extra blankets and clothes. The ward's tile floor was filthy.

MEW interviewed a security detainee in the ward for the care of an infection on the leg. His right leg was covered with dirty rags as bandages which he removed to reveal a dripping sore in the middle of his swollen shin. The sheets and blanket on the bed on which he slept were discolored with dirt. Notwithstanding the appearance of the bedding, he said that the sheets were changed every few days. He also said, in the presence of prison officials who looked on several steps away, that the doctors were very good and that conditions in the hospital were not bad in comparison to those in the overcrowded cells.

The four wards at the Tora Liman prison hospital were generally cleaner than the ward at Abu Za'bal hospital. As at Abu Za'bal, however, patients slept on beds covered in most cases with visibly dirty sheets and blankets. In an upper-floor ward, some patients slept on bare mattresses with no sheets or blankets.

The tile floors of the wards had been cleaned earlier on the day of MEW's visit. Nevertheless, the areas surrounding patients beds, cluttered with the inmates' personal belongings, were covered with dirt. In several of the rooms, MEW found several more prisoners than beds, indicating that some prisoners slept on the dirty floors or shared beds. Prison officials insisted, however, that some of the excess prisoners were in the room only for the day, either waiting to see a doctor in the doctor's office or to clean the hospital wards and washrooms. (This was disputed by one elderly prisoner whom prison officials had identified as one of the men in an overcrowded room who was a maintenance worker and not a patient. But, in a moment alone with this prisoner, pointing to his stomach, he told MEW that he was ill. The old man also did not appear to be the sort of prisoner who would have been recruited for strenuous maintenance work.)

In the rear of one of the second-floor wards were two cells described by officials as "quarantine cells," to hold prisoners who needed to be segregated from others because of their medical condition. These 8-by-10-foot cells were separated from a short hallway leading to the washroom by barred gates. Inside one of the quarantine cells, lying against the far wall, was an inmate, apparently asleep and wrapped in a blanket. This inmate did not stir when a MEW representative greeted him. The quarantine cells had cement floors, damp with muddy water, and lacked the beds and mattresses found in the wards. The walls were dusty and the small two-foot-square window had no glass in it. The conditions in the quarantine room were far worse than those MEW found in the wards. The quarantine cell also was polluted with the stench emanating from the adjacent bathroom (see below).

The single occupied ward at Tanta general prison contained several patients in beds. The beds, however, were covered with the patients' own sheets and blankets, many of which were quite dirty and some of which did not completely cover the patient or provide protection from the night's cold. The floor of the ward did appear to have been cleaned in the past several days, but near the beds and against the walls, where inmates' personal items were stored, the floor was damp and very dirty. The patients' belongings themselves were filthy, as was the room in general.

One patient who was covered with open wounds, described as second- and third-degree burns by the prison doctor, slept in a bed with a piece of foam rubber as a mattress. The foam was filthy and covered with two equally dirty sheets. The patient, who the doctor said was being treated with ointment and antibiotics, "is responsible for his own sheets," according to the doctor. "The patients come with their own mattresses," he added.

Patients' Bathrooms

The washroom adjacent to the patients' ward at Abu Za'bal Liman hospital was filthy. The walls were covered with water, dirt and in some places with mildew and algae. The floors were wet as a result of leaky fixtures and the stalls looked as though they had not been cleaned in some time. A foul smell of garbage, urine, and sewage emanated from the facility. The first of five stalls had a bathtub that apparently was not used. It was covered with dirt, mildew and water and was located in a completely damp room without natural or electric light. Across the short hallway, at the end of which was an inoperative urinal, were two toilet-less stalls filled with garbage, dirt and water. Neither had lights, although one had a large window.

The last three stalls contained toilets. The two on the right contained flat-toilets. Above each flat-toilet was a water spigot, to flush and, higher up, a pipe for a shower. The flat toilets, like the floors of the stalls in which they were located, were damp and dirty. Across the hall, in the center stall, was a conventional, Western-style toilet. It too was damp and dirty. None of these stalls were well lit and all smelled, even though one had a large window. There was running water in all three rooms, but the crude showers dripped continuously. There was no area for hospital personnel to wash, nor any readily available clean towels or bedding with which to accommodate new patients. MEW found no soap or any other products with which hospital personnel or patients could wash themselves.

At Tora Liman hospital, the washroom adjacent to the quarantine cell, in the process of being cleaned during MEW's visit, was nevertheless filthy. There was muddy water which the inmates cleaning the room were attempting to sweep up, but there was no trace of any soap or cleansing solution. There were three stalls, two with flat toilets, and a third with a conventional toilet, lined along the back wall of the washroom. A shower spout in the first stall on the right was the only facility available for personal hygiene. In one corner were four open buckets filled with garbage. The buckets leaked slop onto the wet floor and filled the room with a particularly foul odor.

While the washrooms in the wards at Tora Liman prison hospital were cleaner than the deplorable conditions in the washroom at Abu Za'bal Liman hospital, they were still far from adequately sanitary for a hospital. In addition to the garbage-filled washroom near the quarantine cells, MEW found other washrooms unsanitary. In the washroom in one ward, for example, the two flat and one conventional toilets were without running water with which prisoners could flush them. Prison officers conceded to MEW that patients were forced to take a bucket, walk across the fifteen-foot-wide washroom, fill the bucket with water, and return with the water to flush the toilet.

Like the hospitals at all the prisons MEW inspected, the washroom serving the patients' ward at the Tanta prison hospital was unsanitary and inadequate. There was a single filthy basin in the bathroom with running water. The flat toilets, which were made of white porcelain, were so dirty they appeared dark brown. While there was an upright toilet that was somewhat cleaner, there was no shower or other bathing facility in the hospital.

Other Facilities

• The state of the doctor's office in the hospital at Tanta general prison also raised concerns. Inside, MEW found a bed with a white sheet, a bare examining table, and a desk. There were no supplies and no instruments. There was not even paper to write down anything regarding a patient's problem. The prison doctor attempted to explain that the office is just for first-aid; however, there were no bandages or other first-aid supplies. These, he said, were stored in the pharmacy.[23]

• In Abu Za'bal Liman hospital, next to the ward is a room which the medical officer described as a "temporary laboratory" used for "basic analysis," "under-the-microscope analysis," and "first-aid analysis." The so-called laboratory, which had the appearance of a storage room, contained two desks pushed next to each other against the far right wall, next to a dusty sink, an eye chart, and a dusty, portable partition. There were, scattered about the room, six or seven heavy chairs that looked as if they were being stored there. An examination table, pushed into the near right corner, was covered with dust and appeared unused.

On the desk in front of a large window with dusty curtains was a single microscope. On the window sill were seven dirty test tubes, some in a rack and others simply strewn across the sill. The Medical Director

---

[23]During MEW's inspection of the pharmacy, MEW found six one-pound boxes and nine small cans of infant formula, several dextrose I.V.'s, and a number of dark unlabeled bottles in the several cabinets. Inside the refrigerator there were several boxes of Minophylane and Decongestyl. There were no other supplies readily visible, although there were several locked cabinets.

claimed that an analysis had been conducted in the "lab" just that morning, referring to a log-book, but no supplies for conducting any tests were visible. When asked about supplies, prison officials said that they could not show MEW any supplies because they were locked in the pharmacy and that the doctor who held the key was not available.

While reviewing patients' files in the nurse's office in the second building, MEW representatives were introduced to the head nurse. The office contained files for patients but no supplies. Although officials said prison nurses are responsible for administering injections and changing dressings, the office contained no gauze, tape or other dressing materials. There were no sterile syringes or needles. In a cabinet in the office were several large needles and other medical implements, many of which were broken and rusted, none of which were sterile. When MEW asked where the bandages and other supplies for first aid were kept, prison officials said they were in the now-locked pharmacy. When MEW asked what happened if someone needed first aid after the pharmacy was locked, we were taken to another room called the "dressing room."

The dressing room contained an examination table, spotted with dried blood. The floor apparently had not been cleaned recently. It resembled a storage room; it was filled with furniture, books, and boxes, and the entire room was covered with a heavy layer of dust. Pieces of the ceiling were falling into the room and there was a soiled bedpan next to the door, near a three-foot-high, broken sterilizing machine from which the nurse produced a handful of loose cotton he claimed was used as dressing material. There was no tape and when asked what dressings were bound with, a single small roll of tape was retrieved from the nurses' office.

The second building also contained a tuberculosis ward and an X-ray room. MEW did not inspect either facility, although we were told that the tuberculosis ward held twenty patients from prisons throughout the country.

• At Tora Liman hospital, a low building houses the X-ray room, clinic and pharmacy, as well as a small dusty room with little ventilation and light which prison officials called the physical therapy room. It contained an ultra-sound machine, a stationary exercise bicycle, and several other electric devices which MEW could not identify. There was nothing in the physical therapy room to indicate that the room had recently been used for any purpose. The bicycle seemed to be in working order, but also showed signs that it was not used. None of the electric devices were plugged into the wall and were covered with a film of dirt, apparently formed from dust that had become affixed to the surface with moisture that had since evaporated. The plugs of the electric instruments were also covered with this layer of dirt, indicating that the instruments had not been plugged into an electric source in quite some time. There were no supplies, including no conducting jelly for the ultrasound machine. When asked, prison officials said the supplies were "in storage," although they did not indicate where.

MEW also inspected the clinic at Tora Liman hospital where officials said patients are seen for minor ailments and from which patients are referred to the hospital. The clinic is a small room with two examination tables, a desk, a sink and a refrigerator. There was also a cooking device used, according to a guard, to prepare medicines. However, in the refrigerator, instead of medicine, MEW found cooked and uncooked food. There were a few supplies in the clinic, including several unopened sterile syringes and various bottles of unlabeled medicines.

● While largely indistinguishable from other prison hospitals, the hospital at Mazraa is reportedly only a clinic, holding Mazraa inmates who are primarily treated at Tora Liman hospital. There was an "internist's office" with an oxygen tank, eye chart, and a bed with a dirty blanket on it.[24] There was also a dental office staffed by Dr. Kareem Zahran. Inside, there were several trays with tools laid on old newspaper, a spittoon and dentist's chair, and another bed. In the rear of the hospital were two wards. Several prisoners in each ward were forced to sleep between the beds on filthy cement floors. In the second ward, five of the fourteen patients slept on the floor. In the first ward at least five blind prisoners sat idle on beds among other prisoners with various ailments.

---

[24]The prison medical director, Dr. Kamel, claimed to have slept at the hospital the night before in this bed.

6
WORK AND OTHER ACTIVITIES

"There are no sports. You can only sit or stand. If we try to play, we are disciplined. It is not permitted."

> — *Prisoner in Abu Za'bal Liman, interviewed by MEW in February 1992.*

[I]nmates spent very long idle time in their closed cells. Since they did not work, all they did was to lie down day and night waiting for the next day. Night and day were no different for them, since they had to sleep during both. Such idleness did not help them go to sleep for any length of time, let alone the sixteen hours they were expected to. About seventy-eight percent of drug users said that this had been the main reason for their drug use since they suffered from chronic insomnia due to the length of their nights which started at five o'clock at the latest, and to the fact that they did not use up their energy during the day.

> — *Lawyers Abdallah Khalil and Amir Salem, writing in their 1990 book on Egyptian prisons.*

Idleness is the predominant feature of daily life in Egyptian prisons. This grim reality calls into question the Prisons Administration's stated goal of rehabilitating prisoners "vocationally, spiritually and culturally for their return to society as good citizens and productive workers."[1]   MEW found that only a small percentage of sentenced prisoners were engaged in productive paid work.[2] Further, most prisons offered few alternative activities with which inmates could occupy their time. At only one prison—Tora Mazraa—did prisoners clearly engage in

---

[1] "Humanitarian Care of Prisoners in Egyptian Prisons," undated statement provided to MEW by Prisons Administration officials, February 20, 1992. (MEW translation of the original Arabic.)

[2] In fact, even in the so-called hard labor prisons, or limans, there is no work for the overwhelming majority of prisoners and inmates are idle most of the day (see Chapter One).

physical or recreational training, as required by international standards. To the credit of Egypt's penal system, prisoners are allowed to continue their education on secondary, university and post-graduate levels, although the proportion of inmates engaged in study is small.

WORK AND EMPLOYMENT

At each prison MEW visited, work opportunities for sentenced prisoners, both men and women, were extremely limited. This puts Egypt in violation of international standards, which require that all physically and mentally fit prisoners serving sentences be required to work.[3] The standards specify that "sufficient work of a useful nature...be provided to keep prisoners actively employed for a normal working day."[4] The paucity of useful employment also calls into question a stated policy of the Prisons Administration—that vocational rehabilitation is "one of the important pillars on which the policy of rehabilitating and reforming the prisoners in Egyptian prisons rests."[5]

The existing vocational opportunities consist of agricultural work such as land reclamation and farming, and industrial work ranging from the manufacture of furniture and floor tiles to shoes and apparel. One senior official brought MEW representatives to a large retail store located just outside the Prisons Administration headquarters in Cairo. The store contained well-crafted furniture manufactured by prisoners: bedroom and dining room sets, upholstered sofas and chairs, kitchen cupboards and office furniture, among other items. Also on display were sample floor

---

[3]Article 71(2) of the United Nations Minimum Rules.

[4]Article 71(3) of the United Nations Minimum Rules.

[5]The Prisons Administration further states that employment is aimed at training prisoners "in productive crafts and industries that rebuild the prisoner's self-confidence as a productive member of society ... guarantees him the opportunity for a decent life after his release [and by] paying the prisoner a salary...enables him to purchase things he needs...send a part of this pay to his family...or save part of it." (See "Humanitarian Care of Prisoners in Egyptian Prisons.")

tiles manufactured by prisoners, which could be ordered through the store. Outside the store was a small shop selling shoes, handbags and clothing produced in prison workshops. According to the official, these two stores generated an average of LE400,000 ($121,200) in monthly sales.

Officials told MEW that prisoners received LE50 to LE200 ($15 to $60)[6] per month for their labor, with the salary range depending on the type of work and their own productivity. They noted that skilled workers earned higher salaries. But according to Egyptian lawyers Abdallah Khalil and Amir Salem, wages paid to prisoners are much lower than those cited by officials. In a 1990 report, the lawyers noted that prisoners who work are compensated under three different schemes. First, prisoners in carpentry workshops, while receiving twenty percent of sales revenue from product sales, receive no other salary. Second, inmates in other workshops, bakeries and farms receive wages of LE 2.80 (84 cents) per month, as well as twenty percent of the profit from sales. Finally, inmates assigned to tasks in prison offices, laundries, kitchens, and warehouses receive no wages.[7] MEW did not have the opportunity to confirm current wage rates with prisoners who worked, with one exception. At Tora Liman, a prisoner working on masonry repair whispered out of earshot of the accompanying prison officers: "We are paid LE2.40 (73 cents) a month."

MEW inspected some of the workshops in Egyptian prisons and obtained information from officials about work opportunities for prisoners and rates of pay:

Abu Za'bal Liman: At Abu Za'bal Liman, only about 200 (8.5 percent) of the 2,344 sentenced prisoners were employed. MEW visited a small workshop where handbags and shoes were manufactured. It employed

---

[6]Monthly wages in Egypt average approximately LE 150 for professionals such as physicians, engineers and accountants working in the public sector to LE 150 to LE 250 for their counterparts in the private sector. Workers without higher education earn a maximum of approximately LE 150 monthly and unskilled workers can receive salaries as low as LE 100 a month.

[7]Khalil and Salem, *Prisons in Egypt*.

thirty-one sentenced prisoners, who worked six days a week, from 8:00 a.m. to 2:00 p.m., according to officials. They earned LE 100 to 120 ($30 to $36) per month, their income varying with the quantity they produced. Seventeen other prisoners were employed in a factory that manufactured marble tiles, and another twelve worked in welding and furniture-making. The prison also has a soap-making factory that employed thirty-two men, and a furniture factory that employed 168 prisoners. The director of the Prisons Administration told MEW that the prisoners at the furniture factory worked from 10:00 a.m. to 6:00 p.m. six days a week, and earned over LE 200 ($60) monthly.

Tora Prisons Complex: Gen. Hakim, the commander of the six-prison complex at Tora, told MEW that there are furniture, brick and shoe factories at the facility. He said that prisoners are selected to work in the factories by a special committee in each prison, comprised of the investigation officer and the officer in charge of the factory. The selection criteria include the prisoner's skills, record of good behavior, and the desire to work.

At Tora Liman, according to officials, prisoners worked in furniture, shoes, handbags and brick-making workshops. Agricultural work includes poultry and dairy farming, buffalo raising and horse rearing, and vegetable gardening. At Tora Istikbal, there were no industrial shops, and officials said that the only work opportunities were custodial and maintenance jobs. During MEW's inspection, however, its representatives saw no such workers. At Tora Mazraa, officials said that seventy-eight (under 11 percent) of the 738 sentenced prisoners worked.

Tanta General Prison: Tanta, with 1,803 sentenced prisoners, had only a few small workshops, each employing prisoners who were professional craftsmen as well as unskilled assistants. Twenty men worked in the carpentry shop; ten in basket-making; and four in the shoe shop. Other work was available in the prison kitchen, bakery,[8] laundry, and in maintenance and custodial jobs.

---

[8]Bread is one of the primary products sold outside the prisons, and workers receive twenty percent of the profit generated by the sales. (See Khalil and Salem, *Prisons in Egypt*.)

Officials said that prisoners worked from 8:30 a.m. to 2:00 p.m. every day except Friday, and earned LE10 (about $3) per month. They are drawn from volunteers as well as from prisoners held under "simple work sentences." The prison commander said that inmates are selected for work based on those who express a desire to be employed or "when we need people." He noted that the lack of work was a major problem at Tanta because the prison could employ only some one to two hundred prisoners.

RECREATION

With few work opportunities and the terrible overcrowding, organized sports, outdoor exercise and other forms of recreation become all the more important. International standards specify that prisoners who do not work outdoors should receive at least one hour of exercise daily in the open air.[9] In addition, for young prisoners and those "of suitable age and physique," the prison authorities should provide "physical and recreational training during the period of exercise. To this end, space, installations and equipment should be provided."[10] Yet MEW found that Egyptian prisons do not meet these standards. Notwithstanding prison officials' claims to the contrary, prisons inspected by MEW had no organized physical and recreational training programs, with the exception of Tora Mazraa. At some facilities, active recreation appeared to be limited to a very small number of hand-picked prisoners. Unfortunately, there was little evidence that the Prisons Administration's goal of "filling [prisoners'] free time with athletic activities, and cultural and artistic hobbies" was even close to being achieved.[11]

Physical and Recreational Training Programs

Throughout the prison system, inmates complained to MEW that there were no opportunities for organized sports or other forms of physical exercise:

---

[9]Article 21(1) of the United Nations Minimum Rules.

[10]Article 21(2) of the United Nations Minimum Rules.

[11]See "Humanitarian Care of Prisoners in Egyptian Prisons."

● Prisoners in the Third and Fourth Departments of Abu Za'abal Liman spend time outdoors for several hours daily, but with no organized sports or exercise programs. One prisoner in the Fourth Department said that the men were allowed in the outside courtyard from 8:00 a.m. to 3:00 p.m. daily but "there are no sports. You can only sit or stand. If we try to play, we are disciplined. It is not permitted."

● Sentenced security prisoners at Tora Liman, only recently allowed out of their cells and outdoors for most of the morning, and women in Tanta women's jail, similarly lacked organized sports or exercise programs.

● Prisoners in the atrium-type buildings in the First Department of Abu Za'bal Liman and Tora Istikbal have few opportunities to exercise since they remain confined inside the enclosed atrium section of the buildings. At Abu Za'bal, basketball goals inside the atrium section were dilapidated and not usable. Other atrium buildings had no specific exercise facilities, and Tora Istikbal's Building A was divided by steel gates that precluded even walking around the atrium balcony for exercise.

● At Tanta, where prisoners spend all the time outside of their cells in the interiors of one of two atrium buildings, inmates said that sports such as volleyball are organized three times a week for one hour a day, but "only the teams can play." Team members are, according to inmates, a privileged few selected by the guards. One prisoner remarked that "if you want to play on a team, you have to go to a guard and ask." He said that only about twenty prisoners—out of a total of 2,200 inmates—play sports and that "all the cells watch."

Only at Tora Mazraa could MEW confirm that prisoners were allowed sports or other physical activity. One prisoner said: "Conditions here are relatively good compared to other prisons. We get to go out, play football, basketball, tennis." He added that most of the equipment for these sports was brought by prisoners, calling into question officials' claims that at each prison a specialized office provides sports equipment.

Hobbies

Prisons Administration officials told MEW that, under a "hobby system," prisoners are allowed to make and sell wood carvings, beads, sofa coverings and other items. Prisoners receive ninety percent of sale proceeds, with the balance going to the Prisons Administration. But MEW saw evidence of the presence of hobby shops at only two facilities, Tora Mazraa and Tanta.

Sentenced prisoners at Tora Mazraa showed MEW representatives attractive beaded jewelry and key chains, and exquisitely carved wood plaques with verses from the Koran, all of which they had fabricated. At Tanta, MEW found eleven men at work in a small crafts workshop on the first floor of Building B. Prison officials described it as "a hobby room for both buildings for any artistic purpose." Inmates work at their own expense, supplying materials themselves. Given the size of the workshop, it was difficult to imagine how this small space could serve the needs of some 2,200 men on anything but an extremely sporadic basis.

Reading Materials

Officials told MEW that prisoners are permitted to receive only three Egyptian newspapers,[12] which may be brought to them by their families, or ordered and purchased at the prison. Daily or weekly newspapers published by opposition political parties are not allowed.

"Families are allowed to bring books," Gen. Fakarani told MEW. He added, however: "Political books are not forbidden—but they are controlled." Books were largely absent from most of the cells inspected by MEW, although at Tora Mazraa one group of sentenced security prisoners had put together a small library that contained some 200 books.

In at least one case, prison authorities denied reading materials to sentenced security prisoners. Four prisoners at Tora Liman mounted a legal challenge to the prison's discriminatory policy that had denied them books and daily and weekly newspapers. In a January 1992

---

[12]The three newspapers permitted—*al-Akhbar*, *al-Ahram*, and *al-Gomhuriyya*—are part of Egypt's "semi-official" press and are considered government mouthpieces.

decision, the State Council Administrative Judicial Court ruled that this practice violated Egyptian law and the regulations governing prisons.[13]

Radios and Television

Officials told MEW that prisoners are allowed to have radios and televisions, even in solitary confinement, adding that televisions must be shared and kept in a public place.[14] We saw no radios or televisions in any of the punishment cells we inspected except one: the cell of a woman at Qanater prison who had been condemned to death who had a radio. We did not have an opportunity to ask the occupants of other punishment cells if they had radios in their regular cells. But judging from the lack of *any* personal possessions in most punishment cells MEW inspected, it appeared unlikely that an exception would have been made for radios, much less televisions.

Political detainees held without charge at Tora Istikbal and Abu Za'bal Liman complained that they were not allowed to have radios. And indeed, in their cells inspected by MEW, there were no radios playing or in obvious view. One of the demands raised by the hunger strikers at Tora Istikbal was that the authorities permit radios. In the court case discussed above, the denial of radios to sentenced security prisoners at Tora Liman was ruled unjustifiable and in violation of the law.

---

[13]The court cited Article 30 of Law No. 316 of 1956 governing prisons, which states in part: "Prisoners shall be permitted to bring, at their own expense, books, newspapers and magazines in accordance with what is established in internal regulations." It also cited Article 15 of the Minister of Interior's decision No. 79 (1961) concerning internal regulations of prisons, which stipulates: "*Convicted prisoners...shall be permitted to bring, at their own expense, whatever they choose of books, newspapers and magazines—authorized to circulate—to study in their free time.* The Prisons Administration should examine these books, newspapers and magazines, and should only deliver them to the prisoners after verifying that they contain no violations of the law, do not arouse feelings or the senses or violate security and regulations; sign that this has been done; and stamp these materials with the prison or liman seal. In the event that any of these materials had been prohibited from being printed or disseminated, the relevant authorities and the Prisons Administration shall be notified." Emphasis added.

[14]MEW interview, Cairo, February 20, 1992.

EDUCATION

Officials said that programs exist to eliminate illiteracy, to continue formal education, and to study for university and post-graduate degrees. Few prisoners, however, appeared to take advantage of these programs. According to the Prisons Administration, only 160 prisoners nationwide (a minuscule 0.5 percent of the penal population) were enrolled in secondary-education programs. Of this number, 125 were sentenced criminals. Two hundred sixty-two prisoners (0.7 percent) were enrolled in university studies, 138 of whom were detainees, forty-three of whom were convicted security prisoners and eighty-one of whom were convicted criminal prisoners. Eighteen prisoners nationwide (0.05 percent) were working on post-graduate university degrees.[15] Officials said that under the prison system's education program, course books are provided to prisoners.

MEW met inmates at several prisons who were continuing their education, as well as security prisoners serving long sentences who had earned advanced degrees. But we also took testimony about interference by officials at Tora Liman with sentenced security prisoners who were engaged in academic study (see Chapter Four).

Gen. Fakarani, the director of the Prisons Administration, noted that the authorities undertake efforts to eliminate illiteracy. At Abu Za'bal Liman, officials told MEW that the schoolhouse was used to teach reading and writing to illiterates. They said that classes are held from 9:00 a.m. to 1:00 p.m., every day except Friday, with about thirty students in each of several classes (out of a prison population of 2,463). MEW noted that the door of the school was locked; officials explained that this was "for security reasons." The schoolhouse at Tora Liman, while complete with an outfitted classroom, was dusty and filled with furniture piled into corners as if not used. A similar situation prevailed in Qanater women's prison (see Chapter Seven).

---

[15]These statistics are supplied in "Humanitarian Care of Prisoners in Egyptian Prisons."

Only at Tanta prison did MEW meet a staff member responsible for prisoner education. He said that educational services were provided for about 150 inmates (6.6 percent of the prison's population). He pointed out a sign on a bulletin board in the first-floor corridor of one of the two dormitory buildings. It read: "All who want to take elementary and high school examinations, register and bring papers. The deadline is January 31, 1992."

One foreign-national prisoner at Qanater men's prison complained to MEW that Christian foreigners are not permitted to attend school:

> They made it a rule that one must be a Muslim before one is admitted into the school. Since most of the foreigners are Christians and do not want to renounce their religion, they refuse to allow one to go to the school.[16]

He also alleged that "some foreigners take up correspondence courses with some institutions in Europe, but this has been stopped because the authorities do not allow the books to reach the foreigners here."

RELIGIOUS PRACTICE

The Prisons Administration states that it promotes religion in prisons in the belief that this policy "plays an effective role in correcting the conduct of prisoners and purifying their souls."[17] Activities include the practice of religious rituals and obligations, daily prayer, religious lessons in mosques, celebration of religious holidays, and readings of the Koran. All prisons have, according to the Prisons Administration, one or more preachers for all of the major monotheistic religions to advise and guide prisoners.[18]

---

[16]Letter to MEW dated October 28, 1992.

[17]Ibid.

[18]Ibid.

MEW received several complaints about religious practice from Muslim inmates:

● Palestinian security detainees held in Abu Za'bal Liman said that they were never allowed to pray at the prison mosque or to pray in groups on Fridays, the Muslim day of rest.

● Islamist security prisoners at Tora Istikbal, many of whom endure long-term lock-down, criticized the authorities' prohibition of group prayer during the time outside their cells, on Fridays, and during the feasts of 'Id al-Fitr and 'Id al-Adha.

● Women prisoners told MEW that they never had access to prison mosques. One sentenced prisoner at Qanater complained that inmates were continuously confined to their cells and were not allowed to go to the mosque. Women in the women's jail at Tanta Prison said that they too were not allowed to go to the prison mosque and prayed inside their cells.

● The sentenced "Jihad" prisoners at Tora Liman refused to pray with other inmates in the prison's mosque and did not recognize the *imam* (Muslim cleric) who gave monthly lectures for the prisoners. They demanded that an independent place be designated for their religious practice and daily group prayers. (One of the officers at Tora Liman told MEW that the request to pray in groups was a request for a "special privilege." Prisoners at all other prisons and at Tora Liman pray in groups at prison mosques.) When MEW visited the section of the liman that housed the Jihad prisoners, we found them in the yard that surrounds their cell building. Inside the yard was a large blanket spread on the ground on which some of the prisoners presumably prayed together. The entire Jihad group, however, could not pray collectively since the prisoners are housed in two cellblocks separated by a wall.

The Jihad prisoners pressed their demands in the 1989 lawsuit noted above. The court ruled in January 1992 that although prisoners should be free to practice their religion, this freedom "has its limits and must not violate the prison's order and security." The court found that prison authorities did not prohibit the prisoners from practicing their religion and therefore denied the prisoners' demands for special accommodations for religious practice.

7

CONTACT WITH OUTSIDERS

"With respect to visits, they are not allowed before one month of imprisonment. Visit authorizations used to be obtained at the prison gate, but...the Ministry of Interior now requires that authorizations be obtained [from a Ministry of Justice building in downtown Cairo], creating great difficulties for families coming from distant Upper Egypt and remote provinces."

> *— From a petition written by striking security prisoners at Tora Istikbal, presented to MEW at the prison.*

With the exception of a "quarantine" policy that prohibits family visits for the first thirty days of detention—and sometimes longer for security prisoners—the authorities generally are in compliance with international standards which mandate that prisoners receive visits from family and friends at regular intervals.

As indicated earlier, family visits are critically important to prisoners held in Egypt's penal system because so few necessary items are supplied by the authorities. Families bring prisoners supplemental food, needed medicine, bedding, cigarettes and other basic items. Contacts with relatives are banned during the initial thirty days of detention, due to what officials call "quarantine." After that period, most inmates are allowed to receive regular visits.

According to officials, prisoners under investigation—a category that includes security detainees held without charge—are entitled to weekly visits. Sentenced prisoners, according to Gen. Fakarani, the director of the Prisons Administration, are entitled each month to one "normal" visit, where the prisoner is separated from visitors by a double-mesh screen, and one "private" visit, where the prisoner meets face to face with visitors.[19] (Conjugal visits are not permitted.) In all cases,

---

[19]MEW interview, February 12, 1992.

officials said, requests for exceptional visits must be approved by the Prosecutor General.

Each prison MEW visited had visiting areas consisting of benches in an open yard or hall. At Qanater and Tanta prisons, these areas also included tables. This is where the "private" visits take place; family members are allowed to freely touch and communicate with prisoners. At each facility, MEW saw families waiting to visit their relatives. They carried boxes and bags packed with food, fresh fruit, tea and soda, clothing and bedding, and cartons of cigarettes. The director of Tora Mazraa Prison suggested that allowing families to deliver large supplies of food to prisoners was a benevolent gesture by the authorities: "Rules allow families to bring enough food for only one day, but we allow them to bring more because some prisoners do not eat prison food," he said.[20] One prisoner interviewed in the visiting area at Abu Za'bal Liman said that some of the articles his family brought to him were sometimes confiscated by guards during searches but added that generally this was not the case.

Most visits-related complaints centered on the thirty-day "quarantine" (several prisoners mentioned that they saw their lawyers before they saw members of their families), and on the time allowed for a visit, which inmates said was too short. Based on random interviews at many facilities, MEW learned that the length of time allowed for family visits varies from institution to institution and—sometimes—from prisoner to prisoner. At Tora Istikbal, one security detainee agreed with officials and said that half-hour family visits were allowed once a week. In contrast, prisoners under investigation at Tanta said that only ten to fifteen minutes were allowed for their once-weekly family visits. The commander of Abu Za'bal Liman said that family visits last about thirty minutes, but one Palestinian detainee held in the prison since December 1990 said that visits were only twenty minutes. At Tora Liman, prisoners held in connection with the October 1990 assassination of Parliament speaker Mahgoub said that they received family visits for a half-hour every two weeks in a small room in the presence of prison officers.

---

[20]MEW interview, Tora Mazraa Prison, February 18, 1992.

One sentenced prisoner at Tora Liman, who identified himself as an Islamist, said that non-Islamist sentenced prisoners at Tora Liman received superior family-visit privileges. In a separate interview in a different part of the prison, one secular security prisoner confirmed this. "I have family visits twice a month," he said. "The visits are supposed to be a half-hour, but sometimes I get one hour or more."

Islamist security prisoners at both Tora Liman and Tora Istikbal bitterly complained about the treatment of their families by prison officials during visits. Prisoners held at Tora Liman in connection with the Mahgoub assassination said that their visiting relatives have been verbally insulted by prison personnel, and forced to wait in the sun for up to five hours before being allowed into the visitors' room. A statement presented to MEW by striking detainees at Tora Istikbal noted that families were forced to wait for long periods in unsheltered areas before they were allowed inside for visits. The detainees also noted that authorization to visit detainees can no longer be obtained at the prison's gate but must be secured at a Ministry of Justice building in downtown Cairo. This procedure places an added burden on families who travel from Upper Egypt and outlying provinces: "They are forced to spend the night in Cairo. If they are late and arrive at the prison at midday, their authorization is refused and they are forced to spend another night in Cairo because they will not be allowed to visit until the following day."

Letters

Prison officials told MEW that all prisoners have the right to write and receive letters. Prisoners may receive an unlimited amount of letters, but are permitted to write only four letters a month, according to Gen. Lutfi. He added that a prisoner also has the right to send a letter to his or her family immediately upon arrival at a prison. MEW heard no complaints from prisoners about interference with sending or receiving letters. But because of the high level of illiteracy in Egypt, many prisoners and their families are unable to write, so this form of contact with the outside can be expected to be limited.

Lawyers' Visits

Most prisoners interviewed by MEW had no complaints about access to lawyers. Criminal prisoners under investigation or awaiting trial did not note any problems with access. At Tanta prison, for example, one prisoner in a group of inmates awaiting trial said: "There's no problem seeing lawyers, and they are allowed to stay until they are finished." His cellmates nodded their heads in agreement.

Some security prisoners, however, voiced complaints about lawyers' visits. One detainee on the second floor of Tora Istikbal, for example, said that officers allowed only five minutes for lawyers' visits, making services virtually impossible since lawyers visited three or four detainees at one time.

Lawyers for security detainees must secure permission from the niyaba to visit their clients, which can lead to delays between the time a detainee arrives at the prison and the time he or she first consults with a lawyer.

8
WOMEN PRISONERS

"We are not even allowed to be out to exercise our bodies, yet the rooms are fully packed. Where I am sleeping is 20x60 feet and we are sixty-seven in number. Other rooms are worse off."

> — *Woman inmate serving a life sentence at Qanater prison, writing to MEW in a letter dated November 15, 1992*

Women prisoners in Egypt are held in separate women's sections at general or central prisons, or in the women's prison at Qanater, northwest of Cairo. In fact, in one important respect—long periods of daily confinement inside their cells—MEW found that women inmates at Qanater are treated more harshly than most male prisoners. This chapter reviews the same subjects discussed in the previous sections of this report, but with a special focus on prison conditions encountered by women. The information is based on MEW's inspections of the women's prison at Qanater, Egypt's largest facility for women, and the small women's jail at Tanta general prison, and interviews with inmates at both facilities.

At the time of MEW's visit, the women's prison at Qanater held approximately 1,100—or seventy-six percent—of Egypt's 1,441 women prisoners. Most of the inmates were sentenced criminal prisoners; only about forty to fifty, according to prison officials, were under investigation for criminal offenses. Two of the sentenced prisoners had been condemned to death, one of whom MEW was able to interview (see Chapter Nine).

Qanater women's prison, which occupies slightly more than two acres, is part of a larger thirty-acre facility that includes a men's prison for 2,000 sentenced criminals, which MEW did not visit. The commander of the complex is Muhammed Said Sharawi, but officials told MEW that the women's prison is administered by a woman officer. The women are housed in the oldest part of Qanater, in buildings that were designed by the British and constructed about 100 years ago. The Qanater complex is staffed by thirty-eight officers (two of whom are women), 300 soldiers and guards, and sixteen civilian employees. Inside the women's prison are about eighty women guards, who in all cases are used to escort women prisoners when they leave their cells for any reason, officials said.

In addition to the living quarters, the physical plant of the women's prison includes a separate six-cell punishment wing, a hospital, a library, a kitchen, and an administration building. There is also an industries building, with laundry, knitting and sewing shops. The women's prison buildings are arranged around an open courtyard. In the center of the yard is a group of four buildings, two of which are dormitory buildings. The other two buildings house the prison kitchen, library and laundry. The remaining buildings, built alongside the prison wall, encircle the yard. The administrative offices are near the prison gate in the front of the prison, while the two-story hospital and the punishment wing are in the rear.

The women's jail at Tanta general prison is a much smaller facility, and is physically separated from the men's prison by high walls. At the time of the visit, the jail held, according to the woman officer in charge, seventy-four women, seventeen of whom were under investigation. Among these were seven mothers with their children and three pregnant women. Two of the sentenced prisoners were sentenced to death, but the prison authorities noted that legal appeals were in progress in both cases. As at Qanater, these women were held alone in small cells. The sentenced prisoners were segregated from the women under investigation for criminal offenses.

The jail is in a separate building, with a separate entrance, located behind the prison's administration building, beyond the visiting area. On the other side of a heavy door is a small courtyard, part of which is covered. To the right is the single building where the women inmates are held in six separate cells. On the left, past the covered courtyard, is a small knitting shop and, around the corner, a single washroom. Unlike Qanater, the women's jail was not administered by a woman officer, although it did have only women guards.

INTIMIDATION OF PRISONERS AT QANATER

During MEW's visit to Qanater, there was one serious incident of intimidation of the women in Cell Ten who had attempted to speak freely with a MEW representative. Officers and guards entered the dormitory cell immediately after the MEW representative had conducted an interview with an English-speaking inmate of the large dormitory cell. MEW heard the officers shouting at the women. Another MEW representative returned to this cell some time later, and met with this prisoner. Shielded from the view of guards and prison officials by fellow inmates, the woman spoke rapidly:

> The guards came in and took and tore up his [the MEW representative's] business cards. They asked me what I said and didn't say. I told them that I didn't say anything.

CELL CONDITIONS

Women at both Qanater and Tanta complained about overcrowded and poorly ventilated cells and the oppressive heat during the summer months, particularly troublesome during the times they were confined to their cells. According to the commander of Qanater, the women's prison was originally built to accommodate 500 male prisoners; with its population of 1,100 women, the living quarters therefore were extremely overcrowded (see Chapter Two).

Women at Tanta prison also lived in extremely overcrowded conditions, without sufficient space for sleeping. In one cell, for example, MEW found four women sharing a room that measured approximately 7-by-10 feet. Asked how they managed to sleep in such a small space, one of the women indicated that three of them slept lengthwise and the fourth slept perpendicular to their feet. In another cell, occupied by twenty-seven women and two infants, one prisoner complained: "There is no place to walk when we roll out our mattresses to sleep."

While MEW found the cells at Qanater visibly cleaner than those in other prisons, prisoners indicated that this was due to a deliberate "cleaning up" policy by prison officials. "They have been asking us to clean for the past three days. The white bedsheets you see were not here all the time. They ordered us to get white sheets from home," one inmate told MEW.

"We knew you were coming," one woman inmate at Qanater whispered to a MEW representative. "All the soldiers have been cleaning and sweeping outside for one week." Later during the visit, a prison official told MEW: "Our resources are very limited. In other countries, these buildings would have been torn down long ago. The Prisons Administration does its best to clean and maintain these buildings. Cleanliness is very important to us." When asked to describe the conditions in her group cell, one woman inmate said: "It's disgusting. There are insects, cockroaches and mosquitoes."

Prisoners at Qanater said they had to pay to have bedsheets and other personal possessions washed. "Sheets are taken to be washed for a certain amount of cigarettes," one prisoner told MEW. "For ten packs of cigarettes a month [one pack of Egyptian cigarettes costs LE1.5, or $.50], they'll wash everything." At Tanta, the women did their own wash. Clothes lines filled with hanging laundry were evident in the areas outside the women's cells. Although living cells lacked running water, the communal washroom was equipped with three large sinks.

SANITARY FACILITIES

Women at Tanta complained about the lack of sanitary facilities inside their cells. One 10-by-7 foot cell inspected by MEW had no toilet or running water, and the four occupants were forced to use a metal bucket for a toilet, which they kept in the corner of the small room. They told MEW that the door of their cell was opened at 7:30 a.m. and locked at 5:00 p.m. "We have the pail to use after this time," one woman said, pointing to the corner, "and we empty it in the toilet in the morning." One of the women had been living under these conditions for two years; two other women had been there for for one year. The fourth woman had arrived two months earlier.

Dormitory cells with attached washrooms at Qanater women's prison provided generally more sanitary conditions than MEW found in other prisons, although the overcrowded conditions clearly put a strain on the facilities. But not all the attached washrooms at Qanater were clean.

In the first building inspected by MEW, where prisoners convicted of murder were held, the washroom was filthy and wet. Leaky pipes on the roof and wall showered the floor with water. Algae had grown on the walls and the toilet areas were filthy. Because the washroom was separated from the attached cell by a raised curb, the water did not pollute the living area.

The greater concern in this first building at Qanater, however, was that, of the four cells on the top floor, only one, holding 105 women, had free access to the single washroom. The 121 inmates of three cells on the same floor had no access to the washroom. Prisoners emphasized that they were not allowed out of the cell to use the washroom. Directly across from the washroom, for example, was a small 10-by-15-foot cell holding fourteen women (described earlier). They complained that they were *never* let out of the cell and had to wash and relieve themselves in buckets and with water which one of them collected in plastic buckets and bottles daily.

DAILY LOCK-DOWN

At Qanater, women voiced complaints about continuous confinement inside their overcrowded cells. One cell, measuring about 1,400 square feet, held ninety-nine women. A prisoner who had been there for almost three years told MEW that "sometimes there are over 150 of us in here." She said that the women in this cell were permitted in the outdoor courtyard only about once a month for the count. "The last time we were out of here was about a month ago, for about one hour. We never see the sun. We asked so many times for one hour or even a half-hour outside every day, but," she said bitterly, shrugging her shoulders, "no way." In a separate interview, the fourteen women held in the first Qanater prison dormitory building MEW visited said that they were never let out of their small cell.

One prisoner at Qanater wrote in November 1992 that the cells are "fully packed." She said that sixty-six other women lived in her 20-by-

60-foot cell—providing eighteen square feet per person—and that "we are not even allowed to be out to exercise our bodies."[1]

The inmates in Tanta women's jail fared much better. Twenty-seven women who shared one cell said that the door was unlocked at 7:30 every morning and closed at 4:00 in the afternoon, allowing them access to the outdoor courtyard areas around the cells. The thirty-nine women and four infants in Cell Six had their cell unlocked from 8:30 a.m. to 4:00 p.m. each day. Four women who shared another smaller cell told MEW that they were allowed out of the cell from 7:30 in the morning until 5:00 in the evening. MEW also interviewed one woman sentenced to death, the sole occupant of a small cell along with her one-year-old son. She said that the door of her cell was unlocked from 7:00 a.m. to 4:00 p.m. every day.

DISCIPLINE AND PUNISHMENT

At Qanater and Tanta, MEW encountered no complaints from women about beatings or other forms of gross physical abuse by guards or officers, although at Qanater one sentenced prisoner said that her long hair had been forcibly cut as a form of unauthorized punishment after an argument with a guard. MEW found no women under discipline in Tanta women's jail, but the six-cell punishment wing at Qanater was in use. There, MEW saw harsh conditions and took accounts from prisoners about arbitrary placement in punishment cells as well as prolonged disciplinary confinement.

The punishment wing at the women's prison at Qanater had a locked gate that opened into a barren, dusty courtyard devoid of any objects except a small stone bench. Three cells, each with a faded blue, locked wooden door, adjoined each side of a two-room bathroom which the women used when their doors were unlocked. Cells One through Three each had small peepholes in the door, a little lower than eye level; the remaining cells lacked windows or holes from which to see activity or people in the courtyard. Only three of the cells—Three, Five and Six—had a single light bulb hanging down on the outside of the door. The other

---

[1]Letter to MEW, dated November 15, 1992.

three cells had no source of artificial lighting. A prison official told MEW that the lights outside the cell doors were turned on at sunset and turned off in the morning, but had no explanation about why only some of the cells had light bulbs.

MEW interviewed the occupants of three of the punishment cells: two sentenced prisoners in their twenties who shared one cell; a fifty-year-old Cairo housewife held without charge for security reasons; and a forty-seven-year-old woman who was sentenced to death in 1990.

The two younger women shared one cell that measured approximately ten feet by seven feet. One of them said that she had been confined to the cell for five months, serving a six-month punishment term. Her cellmate had been there for thirteen days. "I was given punishment for six months because I had words with an officer about my mother not being allowed to visit," one of the women said. She has not seen a visitor for the entire five months she has been held in the punishment cell. "No one can visit because I'm in discipline," she said.

The other woman, a university graduate, was there because she had an argument with a female guard. The guard had criticized the prisoner for not giving her cigarettes and an argument ensued. "Cigarettes are a form of money here," the woman said. "The guard cursed me and spoke to me with disrespect. She called me a prostitute." The prisoner said that during the argument, ten other guards came and wrestled her to the ground. Holding her down, they pulled at and then cut her thick black hair. The guard then told an officer that the prisoner struck her and she found herself in the punishment cell.

One of Qanater's six punishment cells was occupied by a distraught fifty-year-old Palestinian housewife, Fathiyya Sayyid Muhammed el-Kurd, who has lived in Egypt for twenty-three years. She was arrested twenty-seven days earlier by State Security Investigation (SSI) officers who came to her Cairo home. She was detained for the first ten days at SSI headquarters and tortured during interrogation.[2] Then

---

[2]Fathiyya el-Kurd's incommunicado detention and torture is discussed in detail in *Behind Closed Doors*, pp. 53-54, 66-67 and 86-87.

she was brought to Qanater and placed directly in the small, barren punishment cell where MEW found her.

She had been held incommunicado and in poor conditions since her arrival at Qanater. "For the first five days, I had no mattress, no blanket, nothing. I just slept here," she said, pointing to the cell's cold cement floor. After five days, she received a piece of foam and a dark grey prison-issue blanket, a gift from other inmates. "No one knows where I am," she said. "My family doesn't know anything. Please let people know about me. Go to the newspapers, bring me a lawyer," she pleaded.

Mrs. el-Kurd had not been out of her cell for seventeen days, and was forced to use the small metal can in a corner as her toilet. "I'm suffocating. I need to see the light. I can't breathe. My head hurts," she complained. She said that she had asked to see a doctor, who came the day before MEW's visit. He merely looked at her through the tiny peephole of her cell's faded blue door: "He wouldn't even open the door. He just said I have high blood pressure and gave me a prescription." Her diet consisted of four loaves of Arabic bread daily and "a little rice and foul or lentils."

MEW raised el-Kurd's case and conditions of confinement at a meeting later the same day with Egypt's Interior Minister, who made telephone inquiries about el-Kurd in the presence of MEW representatives. Several days later, Prisons Administration director Gen. Mahmoud Fakarani denied el-Kurd's charges. Gen. Fakarani told MEW that he inquired with Qanater's prison director, who assured him that el-Kurd "was going to the sun and the bathroom six hours a day. She sees the doctor." Her claim of being held for seventeen days in the punishment cell without going out was "untrue ... it could not have happened," he said. He said that el-Kurd had been assigned a cell in the punishment wing to keep her separate from criminal prisoners. Gen. Fakarani added, however, that after MEW's visit to Qanater, el-Kurd was moved on his order to a separate room in the prison hospital where "she can go into the sun for at least two hours a day."

MEDICAL SERVICES AND FACILITIES

Women prisoners interviewed by MEW did not have major complaints about the medical care they received, although they did note their reliance on their families for the provision of specialized medicines. One woman at Qanater noted that the medical conditions had improved. "I've been here for four years," said one drug offender in her twenties. "The situation has improved. Now the women doctors are good."

The medical officer who directs the hospital said that there are three other resident doctors and a "women's specialist" who comes from the outside. The four doctors on the regular staff are officers in the Prisons Administration and attended the Police Academy after graduating from medical school. The director said that women prisoners receive regular medical exams at their request, and that a doctor regularly tours the hospital, making himself available to discuss medical problems and complaints.

Several prisoners at Qanater noted the problem shared by prisoners throughout Egypt's penal system: dependence on families to bring needed medication. One woman, serving a one-year sentence for prostitution, told MEW: "I have allergies and my father used to bring me medicine. But he hasn't come to see me for a long time, so I don't get my medicine. If you have a family, they bring things you need." Another woman complained about the lack of special medicines, another commonly heard complaint throughout the prison system: "In the summer we get skin diseases and the only medicine they give us is aspirin and salycylics. There are no other medicines here." One woman from an African country, serving a sentence of life imprisonment for narcotics possession, wrote to us about the desperate situation at Qanater women's prison regarding medicine:

> We have doctors but [they] only prescribe medicines. We have to work for someone with a family that comes to see her and give the prescription, as most of us don't have any money. Sometimes you don't get the medicines....We have to serve the Egyptian prisoners who

have families that bring them all their needs in order to survive.[3]

PHYSICAL CONDITIONS IN QANATER HOSPITAL

MEW found the physical conditions in the hospital at Qanater to be far superior to what was observed in other prison hospitals and clinics. The hospital is equipped to handle most emergencies, the medical director told MEW; if not, women have access to the local outside hospital.

The first floor of the two-story hospital contains one ward. The first-floor ward, approximately 25-by-50-feet, contained eleven bunk beds. When MEW visited, there were twelve women occupying the twenty-two available beds. Upstairs, a second, smaller ward, which an accompanying guard called the "sick room," contained seven beds, all of which were occupied. The beds in both wards had clean sheets and the floors of both the cells and the hallways were very clean. The third ward, also on the second floor, contained eight beds. Like the other wards, its occupants wore white gowns and white head scarves. One bed in this ward was unoccupied.

There was only one washroom for the three wards, with a total of twenty-six patients, located on the top floor. There were two flat toilets, one of which was quite wet, although both were relatively clean. There was no shower in the hospital's washroom, and the basin faucets were inoperative. An accompanying guard said that the patients washed either in the wards or in the washroom, using water from buckets. There was no soap evident. Invalid patients, the guard said, relieved themselves in the washroom with the help of fellow patients. MEW saw no bedpans.

There was an operating room, which prison officials conceded was not used. According to a prison officer, only simple medical procedures were performed in the hospital and other operations were conducted in outside facilities. The operating room, like other rooms in

---

[3]Letter to MEW, dated November 15, 1992.

the hospital, was well lit by large windows (that MEW noticed were missing glass).

New patients are initially examined, according to prison officials, in the doctor's office on the second floor. There MEW found bandages, analgesics, and other first-aid equipment. A small medicine closet contained several unlabeled medicines. The room, which was well lit by natural light and a florescent lamp above, was clean.

Pregnant Prisoners and Prisoners with Infant Children

Women who are pregnant when they arrive at a prison give birth in prison or at local hospitals. At Qanater, officials told MEW that normal births are handled by the prison hospital, with deliveries performed by a nurse. If a birth is expected to be complicated, the woman is transferred to an outside hospital, reportedly only two kilometers away. Pregnant women in the women's jail at Tanta are brought to the local hospital to give birth.

The prison commander at Qanater told MEW that there were "about twenty" women prisoners who were pregnant. MEW found that pregnant women, at all stages of their pregnancies, were held in the same cells as their non-pregnant fellow inmates. Pregnant women prisoners at Tanta are held with the other inmates, according to Dr. Rifat Munir Gerges, the prison's medical director.

Inmates who give birth in prison are allowed to keep the infants until the child reaches two years of age. Women who are mothers of infants are also allowed to bring them to prison. Upon reaching the age of two, children are given to the inmate's family if they wish to take them; otherwise, they are placed in an orphanage.

MEW found a wide disparity at Qanater and Tanta between the arrangements for prisoners with children. Qanater women's prison has a nursery, a three-room dormitory building in which twenty-eight mothers lived with their infant children. (Prison officials told MEW that there were forty-five babies in the prison, five of whom came with their mothers, with the rest born in the prison.) The nursery is indistinguishable from any other cell at Qanater, although it was significantly less crowded. All the inmates had a bed to share with their child or children. The nursery's washroom had six toilets and showers, and was relatively clean.

In sharp contrast to the conditions at Qanater, infants and their mothers at Tanta were packed in the same overcrowded cells as other prisoners, and slept in less than ten square feet each on dirty cement floors. MEW inspected Cell Six at Tanta, which was occupied by thirty-nine women and four babies. Two of the children were four weeks old, and two of them were one year old. "There's nothing special for the babies ... nothing," one mother told MEW. This cell is opened at 8:30 in the morning and closed at 4:00 in the afternoon. There is no running water; the only faucet is outside the cell."

WORK AND EMPLOYMENT

Opportunities for work and employment for women prisoners at Qanater and Tanta were extremely limited. At Qanater, there were only three workshops: a needle shop, a knitting shop, and women's clothing shop. Forty-three of Qanater's 1,100 women (less than four percent) worked in these shops. In the knitting shop there were more than ten manual knitting machines and several sewing machines. According to the officer accompanying MEW, the products of the industrial shop were available for sale to inmates in the prison, with the profits going to the women who worked there.

In Tanta women's jail, MEW inspected a small knitting shop which prison officials said they had kept open late for the benefit of MEW's visit. Four women worked in the shop, which has been in operation for only one month. One of the women, who was operating a manual knitting machine, told MEW that she had been transferred from Damanhur prison a month earlier to begin the project and train the other women. She had served sixteen years in prison, and proudly displayed some of the clothing they had produced. She pointed out that the women received forty percent of the profits, after the government subtracted the cost of the raw materials it provided, with the balance going to the state.

EDUCATION

At Qanater there was a small library, the main room of which resembled a classroom. The classroom was not used for formal instruction, according to a prison officer. The officer added that there were no women inmates studying for any degree.

RELIGIOUS PRACTICE

Prison mosques do not appear to be made available for use by women prisoners. Four women sharing a small cell in the jail at Tanta told MEW that they were religious Muslims but that they were forced to pray in their cell: "The mosque is only for the men."

RECREATION

There were no recreational facilities in view for the women in the Tanta jail nor for the prisoners at Qanater. Women at Qanater complained about the long daily periods they were confined to their cells and the lack of time outdoors. "We get no exercise. There are no games. All our muscles are atrophied," one prisoner told MEW.

CONTACT WITH OUTSIDERS

As was the case at other prisons MEW visited, some prisoners said that the time allotted for family visits was too brief. MEW saw the visiting area, which was equipped with concrete benches. Women at Tanta said that they were allowed family visits every fifteen days, and that their children were allowed to come. One prisoner at Qanater said that families are allowed to visit every fifteen days, but that the visiting times ranged from only five to ten minutes. MEW did not have the opportunity to confirm this with prison officials or other prisoners.

Similar to other prisons, MEW heard no complaints from women prisoners about limitations on lawyers' visits or interference with their right to send and receive letters.

CONDITIONS FOR FOREIGN NATIONALS

As with male foreign-national prisoners, women inmates too informed MEW about the special problems they encounter. Because of prisoners' reliance on their families to bring needed items not supplied by the Prisons Administration, women prisoners from other countries who lack means of support are forced to "work" for their Egyptian counterparts, to obtain needed medicine and other items. In November 1992, an African woman at Qanater highlighted some of the problems:

> [L]ife is so terrible in this place for us foreigners. We have no right for anything. We are not allowed any journals. Our letters have to be checked and then taken away for a month for interpretation before they're received. Those not written in English or French are never received at all. In case of parcels, they're received with half of the contents stolen, if you receive it at all. There is no work for one to do for twenty-four hours unless if you are working as a servant to the rich prisoners who only pay in kind.[4]

---

[4] Letter to MEW dated November 15, 1992.

9
DEATH ROW CONDITIONS

"My family can visit only once a month for thirty minutes."

— Woman on death row in Qanater prison.

At the time of MEW's prison inspections, ninety-six inmates, eighty-nine men and seven women, were awaiting execution.[5] Qanater, Tanta and Shibin al-Kawm prisons each held two condemned women, and one was at Minya prison. MEW interviewed the two condemned women at Tanta and one at Qanater (see below). There were thirty-nine condemned men at Cairo's Istinaf prison, nineteen at Tanta prison, ten at Alexandria prison, seven at Minya prison, four at Zaqaziq prison, three each at Shibin al-Kawm and Qena prisons, and two each at Mansoura and Assyut prisons. Gen. Fakarani, the director of the Prisons Administration, told MEW that the last execution in Egypt occurred in December 1991, when three men, convicted of killing a police officer in late 1990, were executed at Alexandria prison.

Capital punishment is not mandatory in Egypt. Under the law, the death penalty can be commuted to a sentence of hard labor for life or for a specific term. Offenses punishable by death include murder in the first or second degree; activities prejudicial to the external or internal security of the state, enumerated in the penal code; torture, arson, the use of explosives and the endangering of public transport if such offenses result in death; the abduction of women if accompanied by sexual assault; perjury if it results in the execution of an individual; and narcotics offenses if such offenses result in death.[6] In recent years, executions

---

[5]Statistics provided by Gen. Mahmoud Fakarani, director of the Prisons Administration.

[6]United Nations Human Rights Committee, Consideration of Reports Submitted by States Parties Under Article 40 of the [International] Covenant [on Civil and Political Rights], *Second periodic reports of States Parties due in 1988, Addendum,* Egypt, CCPR/C/51/Add.7, 2 September 1992, p. 48

have been rare for those convicted of capital crimes.[7] The trend began after the monarchy was overthrown, because "the general atmosphere created by the post-1952 government...was reformative rather than punitive."[8]

Under Egyptian law, the death penalty can be imposed by a criminal court only with the unanimous agreement of the judges and "after seeking the opinion of the Mufti[9] of the Republic. The sentence may be appealed by applying to the Court of Cassation for a review."[10] The law further provides that the Department of Public Prosecutions must submit any death sentence, after it has been presented to the convicted individual, to the Court of Cassation "for verification of the proper application of the law," even if the condemned person does not appeal the sentence.[11] In a final step of review, the law provides that the case file—with the final sentence of death—must be presented to the President of the Republic, who may pardon the individual or use his discretion to commute the sentence.[12] The law states that a death sentence imposed upon a pregnant woman must be postponed until two months after the birth of her child, and that a death sentence cannot be imposed upon juveniles under eighteen years old.[13]

---

[7]*Egypt: A Country Study*, p. 343.

[8]Richard F. Nyrop et. al., *Area Handbook for Egypt*, Foreign Area Studies of The American University, Washington, D.C., Third Edition, 1976, p. 344.

[9]A mufti is an expert on Islamic law, legally qualified to issue decisions on questions of law.

[10]United Nations Human Rights Committee, p. 23.

[11]*Ibid.*

[12]*Ibid.*

[13]*Ibid.*, p. 23-24.

ON DEATH ROW AT QANATER WOMEN'S PRISON

"This is my third year here," Sana Ismail told MEW. The soft-spoken, forty-seven-year-old mother of four was sentenced to death for conspiring to kill of her husband, who was found stabbed to death in their home in June 1989. (Ismail insisted that she is innocent and was forced to confess under torture to involvement in the death of her husband of twenty-five years.) She was sentenced to death on May 5, 1990 and was moved to the small cell in the punishment wing of Qanater women's prison on May 17, 1990.

Cell Five measures about 10-by-7 feet. Like the five other cells in the punishment wing, the cell has no toilet and there is no faucet to supply running water. The only light and air comes from a 2-by-2.5-foot barred window on the rear wall of the cell. The furnishings in Ismail's cell were sparse: a mattress and blankets, a straw mat, some pillows. There were some books and a portable radio.

Sana Ismail told MEW that she is let out of her cell twice daily, for one hour in the morning and one hour in the afternoon, into the open-air courtyard in front of the punishment wing. A metal bucket in the cell serves as a toilet during her long periods of daily confinement. She is allowed visits from her family once a month for thirty minutes.

"If I was a normal prisoner, I could cook my own food. But because I am sentenced to death, I have to eat prison food," she said. She receives lentils, rice or foul, and four loaves of flat round Arabic bread daily. This diet is supplemented by what her children bring on the monthly visits; there was some fresh fruit against the wall of her cell when MEW visited.

CONDEMNED WOMEN AT TANTA PRISON

The two women in the women's jail at Tanta general prison who are sentenced to death enjoy more time outside their cells than their counterparts at Qanater. At Tanta, MEW interviewed Fatima Abdel Hamid Nasr, who said that she was about twenty-five years old and from Cairo. She was in her 7-by-10-foot cell with her one-year-old son Hisham, who was born on the second day of her trial. She said that she has been held in this cell since her arrival at the prison, but that she is permitted to socialize with other prisoners. The door of her cell is opened every morning at 7:00 and not locked until 4:00 pm. The other condemned woman, Nagwa Ali Ismail, twenty-six, is from a small village outside the city of Tanta. Her small single cell had a door with a window and a skylight. The door was unlocked when MEW visited. This prisoner had only two complaints: she said that her family visits her "very little" and that death-row conditions prohibited her from having objects with which she could harm herself or others. "I'm not even allowed to have a sewing needle," she told MEW.

APPENDIX:
PETITIONS FROM SECURITY DETAINEES ON HUNGER STRIKE AT TORA ISTIKBAL PRISON

Some 400 Islamist security detainees were on hunger strike at Tora Istikbal prison at the time of Middle East Watch's visit on February 16, 1992. This was the largest hunger strike organized by prisoners in recent Egyptian history. Numerous detainees provided handwritten notes of protest to members of the MEW delegation. Excerpts from some of these notes follow:

• *A petition signed by "Detained and Tortured at Tora Istikbal" reads in part:*

"We are striking now. Our number is about 400 detainees. Our strike started on Sunday, February 9, because of repeated detention, torture, mistreatment, oppression, poor diet and bad medical treatment. Also because we did not receive blankets, and because of the harassment of our families during their visits to us.

"In addition, they put us in solitary confinement and treat us capriciously. They give us a very short break, without being exposed to the sun. They also do not document our signs of torture when we come from State Security Investigation [SSI]. During the period of detention, they take us for investigation in Lazoughly [SSI headquarters in Cairo] by SSI, which has held us for two years...."

• *A hastily written note, unsigned, provides a list of grievances and demands:*

"Repeated detention, torture and removal to Lazoughly, solitary confinement, nonreceipt of blankets, no openings for ventilation, no break at all for those in solitary confinement, the sun parade.

"What is requested is:
—A break from 8:00 am to 4:00 pm, and on Fridays and feasts
—Permitting books, newspapers, radios, and dried foods to enter
—Allowing permission for family visits to be obtained in front of the prison
—Constructing a shelter for visitors in front of the prison's door

—Allowing the entrance of colored clothes, because it is allowed legally
—Having a doctor permanently in the prison for the patients."

● *One prisoner, who provided his name, said that he was arrested in January 1991 and that his detention orders were overturned eight times by the court. But, each time, he was never set free:*

"I am transferred from Tora Istikbal to Lazoughly, where I am tortured in every release I obtain. They renew my detention from Lazoughly and hold me there for 10 to 15 days. Following that, I am transferred back to Tora Istikbal prison every time, where there is harassment and deprivation of the minimum of my rights as a political prisoner.

"Therefore I demand:
— Supervising of my release by the niyaba.
— Recording the [marks of] torture in the book of the Prisons Administration upon my return to the prison.
— Allowing the entrance of colored personal clothes.
— The break should be from 8:00 a.m. to 4:00 p.m.
— Opening the window in solitary confinement [cells] and allowing them a break.
— Our treatment during the month of Ramadan should be special.
— Improving the poor treatment by the Prisons Administration.
— Improving the medical treatment, particularly in the cases [requiring] surgery.
— The break should be on Friday and the feasts, and the permission to the Friday prayer and the two feasts.
— Extending the time allowed for family and lawyers' visits. The period for family visits should be at least two hours.
— Treating the families well and establishing bathrooms for them.
— Permission to visit should be obtained at the prison's door.
— Allowing the entrance of newspapers, magazines, radios and books.
— Distributing blankets and pillows.
— Allowing "the sun parade" in the prison yard.
— Allowing the entrance of any amount of fresh vegetables."

● *A lengthy unsigned letter complains about prolonged detention without charge or trial, providing the names of eight detainees held since 1990, despite court-*

ordered releases. The letter also describes detainees' grievances relating to prison conditions:

"Among our complaints: bad accommodations and solitary confinement in the basement, which is very cold in winter, very hot in summer, has a sink which floods continuously, and is devoid of any necessities of life. Despite the fact that these cells are meant for punishment, the prison commander insists on confining detainees in them immediately after their arrival at the prison.

"The prison administration does not distribute blankets or mattresses for the detainees, as is established in prison regulations....In addition, they prohibit blankets or plastic carpets.

"Visits are not allowed until after the first month of imprisonment....In the prison area, the families stand for long periods in the cold and the heat without any shields to protect them....Some food is prohibited, such as canned food, greens and dried beans, while at the same time the prison provides extremely bad food not fit for humans.

"The prison administration prohibits collective prayers during the break, on Fridays and during feasts....

"With respect to sun, we do not see it, despite the face that all prisons must allow a period called the "sun parade" from 8:00 am to 2:00 pm. Newspapers, magazines, radios are prohibited.

"Patients and those injured with marks of torture do not receive any attention to their cases. The commander prohibits their presentation to [medical] specialists, which leads to the spread of many skin diseases because of the nonexposure to sun and to influenza caused by exposure to drafts during sleep, and to bone diseases because of severe humidity and the lack of mattresses...."

* * *

Middle East Watch translations of the original Arabic.